Colin Kaepernick:

Modern Day Martyr: In the Shadows of Sacrifice

By: B. Smith, L. Stephens,
M. Mombranche, A. Rivera

ISBN-13: 978-1727319248
ISBN-10: 1727319249

Printed in the USA

DEDICATION

This book is dedicated to Colin Kaepernick, and all of those surrounding the sports world and society who stand against injustice, oppression, and inequality and who refuse to allow the spirit of our great freedom fighters to die. You are true modern-day martyrs: in the shadows of sacrifice!

Acknowledgements

I would like to thank my children, Shae and Joshua, for always being there to support me, love me, and believe in me even when I didn't believe in myself. You both make me a better mother and better person. I would like to thank my mum and dad for always being there to support me and guide me. To my sister, Shirley, thank you for everything. Without my parents and sister, I would never have had the courage or even the inclination to explore such heartfelt and important issues. Thank you also to Caroline, thank you for always being there for me, I am forever grateful. I would also like to thank Patrisse Cullors for acknowledging us, replying to us, and agreeing to write a foreword for us. Sadly, it was not meant to be, but the mere fact that you were able to see and hear us when others didn't means more to all of us than you will ever realize. Lastly but by no means least, I want to thank Magnetic, Sdot, and Saeed. Without these three amazing men I would not have had the courage to contribute to this book the way I have. Thank you for the conversations, the exploration, the support, the knowledge, and your continuous friendship.

-Beverley Smith

Acknowledgements

First and foremost, I thank my Mother, Annette Stephens (RIP,) whose constant, unfailing love I could never lose! Secondly, I acknowledge my son ("Sa'naoz Tolliver") and daughter ("Jai'mika Holmes") whose existence continues to pull me closer to maturity and to the revelations of what it means to be a father. Lastly, I would like to thank Malcom X, Huey P. Newton, George and Johnathan Jackson, and the rest of Malcom's children (i.e., The Black Panther Party) for their courage. I'd also like to thank M. Baruti and John Henrik Clarke, all of whom contributed significantly in started to get me to think! Special thanks to true friends for aiding and assisting the struggle.

--Lorenzo "S-Dot" Stephens

Acknowledgments

First and Foremost, I would like to acknowledge and thank my mother, Esanna Isma, she is the rose that grew from the concrete. I strive for excellence in order to show her my growth and through it all, failures and successes, her love is unyielding. To my nephew Joey Mombranche, who loves me unconditionally, his love is innocent and forces me to think outside of the box about what we must do to get out of the system. I would like to thank all those who work in corrections (Dr. Rodgers, Ms. B, Ms. D, Moore, Big B, Mac, Jack, Hall) and treat those incarcerated as the human beings we are and not less than. I would like to thank my supportive friends, who through my many ideas never stop supporting me, despite how farfetched they may sound (Shantiqua, Fred, Mark, Jerry, Dinu, Mike, Payso, Fresh and so many more). I would love to give a special acknowledgment to my co-authors (who were overly tasked with helping me write this book). First, to "Bev," for being supportive and understanding. The confusing emails, the constant research, the pressure, throughout it all she remained patient. Thank you "mate!" To "S.dot" for the many discussions, build sessions, and stubbornness. I appreciate it.

Last but not least to the "perfectionist," the big brother, the chief editor, "Saeed," without you a lot of this wouldn't be possible. If it were up to you, we would still be editing this book! Thanks, my brother. I would like to acknowledge Patrisse Cullors (B.L.M Co-Founder) for answering the call from the hundreds who were asked to contribute a foreword. She is the real deal, with all she has going on such as activism, school, and life, she sought to make time. Though activism called and our schedules were unable to coincide, thanks for not judging us. Most importantly, my "NOGE" Family and Father "ALLAH" (Clarence 13X) for his manifestation of "Lessons" which gives me my foundation to build upon. Peace, Proper Education Always Creates Elevation. To the many Martyrs around the world who stand, sit, kneel, fight, die, encourage, and inspire, this book is a testament of that never-ending spirit that causes new leaders to rise and fight for the people!

-Mikey "Magnetic" Mombranche

Acknowledgments

First and foremost, I acknowledge the Great Spirit of Life, Wakan-Tanka, Amun, Tao, Olodumare, Allah, GOD that resides within me and is expressed through my physical faculties in which I (GOD) now reside.

I pay homage to my ancestors, in particular my grandfather Mateo; my grandmother "Paca" for giving life to my Earth/queen mother Providencia Latifah Rivera; and to my father Willie Rivera thank y'all for passing the gift of life on to me. To my daughter and queen, Saeeda Latifah Daniels-Rivera I love you with all my heart and anything I will ever accomplish is for you. To my big brothers Khalil, Bee-Chee, Jamal, and my big sis Aisha I love y'all no matter what. To all my family, Lil' Aisha, Najma, Muhammad, and Michelle and friends that have been there for me in times of need, thanks and love to y'all. To my aunt Bilquis (RIP) you will never be forgotten, "Umie" you meant the world to us. To my son, Bilaal: the external condition of a man will not change unless, and until, he first changes the internal condition of himself. To Kenah and Nathifa thanks for making your mother proud, y'all are the products of her hard work and discipline. To sister Bahiyah, thank you for giving me my children and always keeping them in my life under all circumstances. Y'all already know how much I love ya'll. I would be remiss if I did not extend my gratitude to Mrs.Grant for the encouragement and good deeds; thanks for remaining true to the human character of compassion...Blessings. Also, thanks to Mrs.Gordon and Mrs.McClary in EDU for the continued efforts in rehabilitation and education in the lives of many, the world is a better place with people like y'all.

To all those greats of the past and present that have been influential in my personal and spiritual growth: Ausar & Auset, The Orishas, Prophet Muhammad & the Four Caliphas (Abu

Bakr, Uthman, Umar, Ali,) Imam Ali & the Twelve Imams, Lao-Tzu, The Buddha, Honorable Elijah Muhamad, Malcolm X, Min. Farrakhan, Clarence 13X, Marcus Garvey, Haille Selassie I, Warith Deen Muhamad, Martin Luther King Jr, The young Lords Party, The Black Panther Party, Sioux Medicine Man Black-Elk and the Taino Nation past and present. I thank y'all for your wisdom and guidance in my life journey.

Special thanks to my co-authors. Bev, what would we have done if the universe had not set the cornerstone, the female aspect in place? GOD is not complete without the pillar being set in place so that the temple can stand upon firm ground. Thank you for listening to your calling. To "S-Dot" thanks for helping me understand that we could not have done anything without each other's minds being on one accord. The work could not have been perfected if you weren't in those long, grueling sessions! Power to the people! To "Magnetic" your vision has been manifested. Keep thinking and coming up with ideas, GOD! Everything begins in the mind. You already know that "Allah's Mathematics Makes the Cipher Complete" so: creation consists of four (4) essential elements: fire, air, earth, and water. "Magnetic" or "magnetism" corresponds to FIRE, in Yoruba (IFA) "shango" =god of fire, thunder (Magnetism) also equates to lighting and drums which represent constant rhythm, dance and music

Movement! Action! Thus, when you do the knowledge you SEE yourself in the science of life... GOD manifested, A.L.L.A.H.; so, don't trip if they think you can't stay still... or that you are constantly moving! Peace, lil' bro.

--Saeed Rivera

CONTENTS

MARTYR:
A person who suffers or is put to death for refusing to renounce a faith or belief; [a] constant sufferer.

PROLOGUE

"Man, I got a vision!"
--Mikey "Magnetic" Mombranche
(The words that were uttered that gave life to this book)

The idea for the writing of this book came about as a young man sat in federal prison, absorbing the current events unfolding in his society. The events were played out through television, news coverage, newspaper, magazine articles, books, sporting events, schools, talk shows, and campuses across America. The conversations ran rampant, unfolding relentlessly, and it seemed as if a wildfire had been lit. In the midst of the chaos, Mikey "Magnetic" Mombranche received a vision.

The story behind Colin Kaepernick's decision not to stand for America's national anthem during N.F.L games gave rise to Magnetics vision. His fascination with the chatter surrounding Kaepernick's stance and the underlying causes Kaepernick based his stance upon, fueled Magnetic's desire to set forth a conversation in the form of a book, which would help substantiate Kaepernick's decision to protest injustice and oppression inflicted upon black and brown peoples all across America. After recruiting two of his trusted comrades within America's new plantation system (prison,) Lorenzo "S. Dot" Stephens and Alfred "Saeed" Rivera, and his beautiful sister Beverley Smith (thousands of miles away in Germany,) Magnetic commenced upon a mission to manifest his work.

***

For many, the painful reality is that prison life can shatter the soul and will of anyone who experiences it. It can destroy thought utterly. In contrast, for some, the dreadful prison environment works towards sharpening the wits and strengthening the will to evolve the soul; it works towards removing the veil of ignorance, revealing light to the intellect that one begins to see clearly though surrounded by darkness.

This book is the result of a "War" that waged within the psyche of a twenty-three-year-old black male over a course of a few years. This war was a mental one being fought from within, in an attempt to dispel the notion that the degenerate societal conditions plaguing black and brown peoples and their communities were due solely to their own lack of will or desire to do and have better. He could not come to terms with such a notion. It was at this juncture in his life that Magnetic began an intense investigation into the history of America, her treatment of black and brown people throughout her history and the ills that continued to plague her for centuries. The veil had been lifted and America had exposed her shame to him.

During the first few years of Magnetic's incarceration

his time was filled with self-reflection, self-analysis, and a search for purpose in life. As he matured, he began to realize he was a product of his environment. An environment sweltering with the heat of poverty, drugs, and crime, and that America's turbulent history played a significant role in the degradation of black and brown lives as presently witnessed in this twenty-first century. He now understood that his condition, the condition of his community, and the overall condition of black and brown people in America, was not created within a vacuum but in fact was a condition created by way of an implicit, racist system designed to impede the growth and success of black and brown people throughout this entire nation. His own personal transformation culminated into a rational-thinking individual, capable of identifying those issues disproportionately affecting him, his community, and black and brown people at large. The issues he began to identify were identical to those Kaepernick's stance was premised upon. This was enough for him to join the fray.

***

As the vision for the writing of this book materialized, the atmosphere in American society became reminiscent to the past, saturated with the vitriol of racism and hate. The 2016 drama-filled battle between Hillary Clinton and Donald J. Trump showcased a circus of candidates vying for the hearts and votes of all Americans. The anxiety experienced by many was on par to the anxiety felt by those who lived through the dark periods of America's history when racial hatred and bigotry was the norm. As Donald J. Trump played to the tune of hatred and divisiveness, many Americans were manipulated by his demonic melody. Trump was able to play a tune placating the fears of many, using their weaknesses to convince them that America must return to her dark past in order to become "Great Again." In this atmosphere, Kaepernick's stance emerged. In this atmosphere, this book had begun to be discussed.

Just as America watched her first African-American President, Barack Hussein Obama, serve and complete his second term in the White House, she subsequently watched as she swore in her first openly racist demagogue. Race and justice were once again front and center as each side of the debate became entrenched in its own rhetoric. It was at a point that the notion of an all-inclusive America that the Obama Presidency had alluded to, was proven to be nothing more than rhetoric itself. The writing of this book was borne out of this reality.

The contents of this book represent a wake-up call toward the importance of social and civic engagement by the people for the upliftment of the people. The struggles of the people to secure freedom, justice, and equality for all is paramount even in this day and time. The writing of this book is an awakening to the fact that Kaepernick is just another martyr for this modern day in the shadows of sacrifice...

Alfred "Saeed" Rivera
November, 2017

Introduction

"What happens to a dream deferred?"
does it dry up
like a raisin in the sun?
or fester like a sore ----
And then run?
Does it stink like rotten meat?
or crust and sugar over ---
maybe it just sags
like a heavy load
or does it explode?
--"Harlem (A Dream Deferred)"
by Langston Hughes

It is fitting to commence the introduction of this book with a poem, "Harlem (A Dream Deferred,)" written by Langston Hughes during a time in America where it was very clear that separate was not equal. Hughes knew his ancestors waited many years and did not experience true equality, and he wondered whether or not he ever would. Today, many Americans hold the same sentiments as Hughes did.

The writing of this book draws from the iconic stance of Kaepernick at a time in America when his generation remained disillusioned, despite the many gains their ancestors lived, fought, and died for in an attempt to ensure that America lives up to the ideals which her freedom fighters envisioned for all of America's children. In Kaepernick's story those "dreams" that Hughes wrote about still seem distant, even over a half century later. Those hopes, ideals, and goals that can give life its purpose are still desired, even to this very day.

***

In the pursuit of freedom, justice, and equality, a pursuit woven within the seams of America's turbulent history, the dreams and aspirations of the people have always given rise to various forms of resistance. In the pursuit of these ideals, many have suffered martyrdom. In the pantheon of American heroes, many have been reviled and dismissed as irresponsible trouble-mongers; their only "crime" being that they resisted oppression and were intent on paving a path towards freedom and dignity for all. Only later would these individuals be vindicated and raised to iconic status, either when it became politically correct or expedient, whether in their lifetime or posthumously. In line with this occurrence, Kaepernick, too, will one day be vindicated; his bold stance remains as a testament to his true purpose in life.

Kaepernick stood at the margins, deliberately challenging America and her hypocrisy. He stood so that maybe society, as a whole, would be ready to join him in acknowledging, arising, and taking action in this very old, very long struggle to capture justice and freedom for all. Today, Kaepernick has challenged America to continue building upon the foundation previously laid by countless others who sacrificed their time, energy, possessions, and in many cases their very lives, that all Americans may truly become free and equal.

***

In light of America's shameful past, remnants of which she still struggles to rid herself of, there is nothing surprising concerning Kaepernick's bold stance. At every juncture of America's existence, her children have stood up in an attempt to ensure that the demands of freedom are secured for all. Today Kaepernick is one of these children, treading the path of his forebearers, understanding that America's many noble and honorable gains were not in vain.

As America plots a steady course towards her true glory, she will no doubt encounter turbulent winds; just as oppression and inequality continue to emerge in various new forms, so will resistance, and countering oppression from every angle. We contend that Kaepernick's stance is an example of these "new forms" of resistance which will emerge as the thorn in the side of injustice and oppression as long as they exist in our society. Herein, we contend within the confines of reasonable discourse that the very dreams Hughes wrote about, those dreams Dr. Martin Luther King Jr. based his iconic speech upon, are the same dreams which have now inspired Kaepernick to protest in the manner he has chosen.

***

The writer Jesus Colon once penned: "...to deserve a people's love... you must learn to appreciate their history... their aspirations for human advancement and freedom..." From the early years in America when most indigenous Native Americans were experiencing the effects of genocide and most blacks still lived in slavery, despair over the conditions of their lives had burst periodically into efforts to relieve those conditions. Today, in observing oppression and injustice, Kaepernick chose to confront America in the same vein as those illustrious warriors, freedom fighters, abolitionists, and civil rights advocates before him: boldly! How, then, could this generation of Americans not understand his courageous stance?

Indeed, America must come to terms with history. She must be able to look history in the face and then critically examine the notion that all is well; as much as America has gained, we owe ourselves and the world much more. When we expose the claims and denials of those who oppose freedom, justice, and equality to the heat of historical analysis, we then fortify the stance of those who sit, kneel, stand, and protest in opposition to the infringement upon basic human rights and freedoms. The writing of this book is an attempt at such an exposure.

The subjects taken to task in the chapters of this book present an opportunity for Americans, and the world, to objectively and impartially weigh the history of oppression against the existing remnants of oppression. Injustice continues to permeate American society in this twenty-first century, even after centuries have passed since Europe entered the Western hemisphere, destroying everything in sight. As one attempts to capture the various influences and underlying causes that have given rise to Kaepernick's protest, the subjects herein act as a guide, shining a light on footprints left upon a trail; a trail littered with the footprints of imperialism, colonialism, genocide, slavery, and injustice. All of which continue to castrate black and brown people, as well as other minorities all across America.

***

In the shadows of the chatter surrounding Kaepernick's stance, the unspoken question facing America is: how did we come to let this pass? Some of the answers, albeit unsatisfactory, are such that all too frequently tragedies concerning black, brown, and poor people continue to burden our society, stretching back centuries. America's story cannot be detached from the reality of deprivation which gave rise to the degradation of people as witnessed in the ghettos, inner cities, towns, and Native American reservations of America. It is a story which began hundreds of years ago, beginning with the genocide and enslavement of people, the rape and colonization of an entire hemisphere, followed by the subsequent systemic injustices that continue to cripple later generations of Americans. It is a story that runs through so-called Indian Laws, Reconstruction, Jim Crow, de jure and de facto segregation, decades of neglect, economic instability, undereducation, the Prison Industrial complex, and mass incarceration (to name a few.) These undeniable, centuries-old, historical and generational underpinnings are central to the current rationale for protest taking place all across America by Americans of every race, creed, gender, and background.

***

The problems of racial bias in our society remain intact, subtly infecting every generation up until this very day. The residue of oppression is painfully real, challenging our nation every step of the way. Today, we are constantly reminded of the subtle ways in which our past misdeeds continue to infiltrate our society; a society refusing to fully submit to the wisdom of those ideals we claim to stand upon. As Samuel Adams so eloquently put it:

"The sum of all is, if we would most truly enjoy the gift of heaven, let us become a virtuous people; then shall we both deserve and enjoy it. While, on the other hand, if we are universally vicious and debauched in our manners, though the form of our Constitution carries the face of the most exalted freedom, we shall be the most abject slaves."

To begin to address the vestiges of racism and truly become a "virtuous people," would be to remedy, at least in part, the broader social conditions that have produced poverty, undereducation, economic instability, housing inequality, inadequate healthcare, and a multitude of conditions that continue to undermine the social progress of black, brown, and poor people in America.

The call seeking to galvanize the People towards social reform, justice, and equality has been made. Kaepernick has made a sacrifice for this generation in daring to make this call. There can be no doubt that Kaepernick's stance has provided American's an opportunity for constructive dialogue. The reality is that, in America, the conversation in relation to race and justice has been avoided for far too long. At least now, we can concede that Kaepernick's protest has forced us to engage in this conversation. The fact that people are brought together by considering the point of view of others is sufficient reason for America to openly invite this conversation, and though we all may not agree on Kaepernick's method, we should respect the basis of his mission.

Kaepernick's stance against oppression has, indeed, disturbed many. However, the necessary change regarding issues that desperately plague our society cannot be relegated to the backseat, placating society's minority, to the detriment of a burgeoning majority who are ready to tackle the issues head-on. Kaepernick's stance has prompted many Americans of all backgrounds to raise critical questions regarding issues pertinent to an equal and just society. This is a good thing, as his stance has led to conversations involving a multitude of topics: community issues, race relations, racial injustice, prejudice (in all areas of our society,) police relations, education inequality, gender inequality, economic inequality, housing inequality, military pride, patriotism, inadequate veteran's assistance, and a host of issues relevant to the concerns of everyday Americans.

***

Kaepernick's protest began in an attempt to highlight the social ills plaguing America. The lingering misgivings of her past that her children now seek to rectify, and Kaepernick is one of these children. How can we blame Kaepernick and still claim that we cherish the sacrifices of those of our past who have similarly sacrificed the comforts of life, seeking to highlight injustice? When do the aspirations for justice and human advancement become a reality that America's children may live in peace after all? Why do her children remain at the crossroads on issues concerning race and justice though many have sacrificed in the interest of a greater, more inclusive America? Should not this generation be reaping the benefits of the many sacrifices of yesterday and today? These are the pertinent questions that give rise to the spirit of protest exemplified in one N.F.L. player who sat quietly upon the altar, ready and willing to sacrifice himself for a greater cause and unless America submits to her lofty ideals, he will not be the last or only child to be offered as the proverbial sacrificial lamb.

The vilification of Kaepernick has backfired, as many have been inspired by his sacrifice. The attempts to discredit him and trivialize his stance have only caused many to become informed as to the basis of his protest. The writing of this book is a step towards Colin Kaepernick's vindication. It is also an open invitation to examine those truths and realities (historical and present) that caused a young N.F.L player, well on his way to greatness on the field, to sacrifice for greatness off the field.

As truth always prevails in the end, so shall Colin Kaepernick!

Alfred "Saeed" Rivera

Chapter 1

Colin Kaepernick

*"I am not going to stand up to show pride in a flag
for a country that oppresses black people and
people of color."*

--Colin Kaepernick;
Pro Athlete, Activist, Icon.

Colin Kaepernick was born on November 3, 1987 in Milwaukee, Wisconsin. Colin's biological father was African-American, and his biological mother was white. While still a baby, Colin was put up for adoption and was soon adopted by a married couple, Rick and Teresa Kaepernick who were already raising two children when they brought Colin into the fold of his new family.

Colin Kaepernick grew up with two siblings, a sister, Devon Kaepernick, and a brother, Kyle Kaepernick. The Kaepernick children grew up in an environment of diversity, tolerance, and compassion; qualities that would later be exemplified in Colin's own life.

Early on in Colin's youth, he began to show that he was athletically inclined and put those talents to use by playing football. Specifically the quarterback position, due to his strong arm. By his high school years, though obviously talented, scouts were stand-offish by what they had deemed Kaepernick's awkward throwing style and less-than-perfect accuracy. In college, these doubts about Kaepernick's abilities would began to dissipate on October 6, 2007 with the "Wolf pack's" (University of Nevada, Reno) home game against Fresno State. In that game the "Wolf Pack's" starting Quarterback, Nick Graziano, suffered a foot injury and it was Kaepernick that would step up and lead the team, throwing an incredible 384 yards and scoring four touchdowns! Needless to say, Kaepernick became and remained the "Wolf Pack's" starting QB.

It was Kaepernick's on-the-field performances that led the N.F.L's San Francisco 49ers to pick Kaepernick in the 2nd round of the 2011 N.F.L draft. After the 49ers then starting QB, Alex Smith, suffered a helmet hit to the head in their November 11, 2012 game versus the St. Louis Rams, it was yet again Kaepernick's turn to lead his team. This ultimately led to the San Francisco 49ers Super Bowl appearance!

However, despite Colin Kaepernick's electrifying performances and quick rise to fame as the San Francisco 49ers starting QB (as Alex Smith would never recover the starting position,) it would be his bold stance, using his N.F.L platform against racial injustice and inequality that would bring him the most fame... and as a consequence, the most criticism.

***

In August of 2016, as the national anthem played, Colin Kaepernick kneeled in protest of America's ill-treatment of black and brown minorities. For his monumental stance and the subsequent movement and awakening it stirred, Kaepernick was, for all intents and purposes, "Black-Balled" from playing in the NFL. However, in all great matters of importance, an equal amount of sacrifice is always necessary. For Kaepernick, the desire to express himself and take a stance against injustice came with a price. He would have to pay the sum of sacrifice, he would join a prestigious group of humanitarians who had already given much in hopes that the pains of their labor would produce a harvest for the multitudes to enjoy.

For centuries, race and justice have struck a nerve in America. The issues relating to the fight for justice and equality have deep roots in our society. There have been many men and women of various races, creeds, and backgrounds who have made sacrifices in some form or another in this long fight. Kaepernick has continued this tradition and chosen, albeit unwittingly and unknowingly, to make a sacrifice and follow the footsteps of those before him. Although his sacrifice may not be appreciated by society or those who may benefit from it, it is nonetheless necessary in the effort to bring forth a greater good. We can be assured that Kaepernick has made the right choice in sacrificing his beloved career, despite being vehemently ridiculed and lambasted, in the face of staring down the lingering injustices prevalent in our society.

***

Many have suggested that Kaepernick "...threw his football career down the drain," that he has caused himself "...to lose millions of dollars," and that he "should just play football"; while others simply believe that "...he has disrespected the flag." Although it seems that many have considered the finances and weighed the logic behind their opinions of Kaepernick, it is abundantly clear that many have failed in considering the root causes of the issues that plague black and brown people in America. Then again, maybe many have considered, but stubbornly refuse to acknowledge the gravity of the issues that have propelled Kaepernick to sit, kneel, and clench his fist in protest. Could it be that maybe some just refuse to acknowledge the crippling effects of racism, poverty, police brutality, killings, and the systemic oppression lingering in our society and just want to "enjoy the game?" Do we blame Kaepernick because he chose to acknowledge and act?

By taking this stance, Kaepernick has shouldered a fight on behalf of the voiceless, using his platform to continue a mission on behalf of the oppressed just as many before him have. Today, as many of us would love to just enjoy the game, many of our fellow Americans remain marginalized, disenfranchised, and in far too many cases, brutalized by those chosen to "protect and serve" us. Is this enough to interrupt our game?

***

Colin Kaepernick took a stance in an attempt to express the realities that are oftentimes excluded from our conversations of race and justice. Indeed, a deep-rooted problem exists in America, a problem that goes beyond the fact that poverty, crime, violence, mass incarceration, police brutality, and drugs are real. Kaepernick's stance and the people's voices seek to reach the core of this problem, and as long as our institutions (government) and corporations (such as the N.F.L.) condone or turn a blind eye to racism and injustice, then these same entities should expect protest as the people attempt to obtain redress. If we, as a nation, continue to avoid the conversation then we must expect protest whether in stadiums, arenas or on the fields of the N.F.L., the people's voices will not diminish in the face of racist rhetoric or to simply "get on with football and play the next down."

Despite the hate, vitriol, and negative publicity that has followed Kaepernick, he has much to gain. It is said that "a man's quest for gold is his undoing." Thus, it may be fitting that Kaepernick has sacrificed his "gold" for the greater good of his country. In this, he can be assured that when his chapter is closed, he will have been elected into that "Great Hall of Fame" that many illustrious greats before him reside, such as Barbara Easley Cox, Sojourner Truth, Stokely Carmichael, to name but a few. This "position" in life can never be taken from him, nor can he be "black-balled" out of it!

CHAPTER 2

RESISTANCE: In the Spirit of Freedom

"Let your motto be resistance!
resistance! RESISTANCE! No oppressed
people have ever secured their liberty
without resistance."

--Henry Highland Garnet,
(1843)

Resistance was born from the womb of freedom. Africans, Native Americans, and their descendants have found themselves resisting since the inception of Europe's attempts to conquer and colonize and thereafter introduce its diabolical slave trade into the continents of Africa and North and South America. Their resistance has always been in opposition to kidnapping, captivity, enslavement, rape, oppression, and genocide. The focus of their resistance has always been to regain the freedom and dignity so wrongly stolen in the name of imperialism, colonialism, and supremacy. This spirit of resistance has remained, to this very day, engrained in the psyche of the descendants of Africa and Native America. Resistance was, and remains, the natural result of the darkest crimes mankind has ever committed against his fellow human beings. Crimes of which the human imagination still cannot fully fathom: The African and Native American Holocaust, the genocide of millions of innocent souls. "Hitler's concept of concentration camps as well as the practicality of genocide owed much, so he claimed, to his studies of English and United States history. He admired the camps for Boer prisoners in South Africa and for the Indians in the Wild West; and often praised to his inner circle the efficiency of America's extermination–by starvation and uneven combat–of the red savages who could not be tamed by captivity."

—John Toland

It is by nature that the humblest of creature will eventually strike back when faced with the preservation of its right and will to exist unburdened by the whims and desires of an oppressive force, intent on its demise. Therefore, resistance is not such a rarity in the face of oppression or in the face of the infringement upon one's inherent right to life, freedom, justice, and equality.

RESISTANCE IN ANCIENT TIMES

Resistance covers a vast majority of the narrative in the annals of world history. As far back into antiquity as Egypt's 18th Dynasty (1549-1292 B.C.,) the Pharaoh Ahmose I, drove out invaders and colonizers (the Hyksos) after centuries of foreign and oppressive rule. A rule, which set in motion the destruction of cities and temples and led women and children into slavery. Continuous periods of resistance during the coming centuries finally expelled the invaders, along with all traces of their occupation, out of Egypt. All nations and societies of the world have been tested, in some form or another, with oppression, colonization or domination. As a result, world history provides innumerable examples of the people's desire and will to stomp out such evils utilizing resistance.

Even the once mighty Roman Empire records in its history the story of the Thracian gladiator Spartacus, who after escaping Rome's gladiator schools using kitchen utensils as weapons, commanded a massive slave army. Slaves from across the Roman countryside soon joined his revolt, defeating militias and legions of Roman soldiers who were hell bound on keeping people enslaved by inflicting unspeakable pain and suffering on them. This uprising went down as the largest and most successful slave rebellion in Roman history. The anger provoked by a life in chains, under oppressive rule, has often spilled over into violent revolt and uprising. Such results are not uncommon in the face of such circumstances.

RESISTANCE IN AFRICA

Long before Africans were kidnapped and brought to the Western hemisphere, they had already experienced resistance in the Middle East, eventually going head-to-head with an empire. In 869 A.D. the Zanj Rebellion saw East Africans rise against the Abbasid caliphate along with the Arab revolutionary, Ali Bin Muhammad, amassing an army that supposedly reached a strength of 500,000. Raiding cities, seizing supplies, and liberating fellow slaves along the way, the people fought a revolution that lasted nearly two decades.

In 1442, Portugal began to kidnap Africans, take them out of Africa, and enslave them. The Portuguese enslavers arrived on the shores of Africa, disembarking from their ships equipped, armed, and ready to capture or slaughter the unsuspecting innocents. Before long, the African population wised up to the intent of the Portuguese and began incorporating various methods of resistance to counter the onslaught. There were three predominant ways to demonstrate resistance against slaveholders, they would rebel, run away or make a conscious effort to slow down work on a daily basis.

Oftentimes no match for the guns and canons of the Portuguese, the people nevertheless remained resilient in their efforts to resist. Resistance was a natural response as Portugal attempted to introduce its evil trade upon the African continent.

One of the most important accounts of resistance against Portugal came in 1595, The Revolt of Amador, named after the revolutionary that instigated the revolt. On the controlled island of Sao Tome a rebel army of up to 2,000 enslaved Africans attacked the city, burning factories and farms to the ground. The people fought relentlessly as they sought to recapture their freedom from the hands of the oppressor. Days into the rebellion up to 5,000 rebels stormed the main city, massacring and destroying all in their path. The fiery need to be free and live with dignity can never be extinguished. After years of enslavement animosity, frustration, and hatred lead to this revolt and the people felt compelled to achieve their freedom by any means available to them. It is the nature of humanity to resist when faced with the infringement upon these indelible rights. And though the results of resistance are oftentimes gory, resulting in physical violence, rape, torture, and often death the necessity remains in order to win the freedom of those held in bondage.

History narrates that the conquering invader is never left to rest easy when the people remain vigilant in their quest to be free; Portugal's rule on the African continent accompanied by centuries of resistance is one more example of this. One of Africa's greatest leaders, born into the struggles of her people, was Queen Nzinga (1581-1663) of Angola. Queen Nzinga would live a life of resistance that stretched thirty years. Born in 1581 in the Kingdom of Ndongo, Nzinga would grow up watching her people go to war with the Portuguese until she would eventually lead the people in war against the slave trade and European influence. Offering refuge to escaped slaves, encouraging revolts among Africans against the Portuguese, and eventually forming alliances with neighboring groups Nzinga was able to influence her people and command their respect, thus furthering her ability to resist. Today, her legacy endures throughout Africa and the world as a true testament to the spirit of resistance.

There is a desire that burns within the oppressed to secure their inherent rights, and this desire has been ablaze for centuries. This eternal blaze may weaken at times, but it remains lit as the torch is continuously passed on to subsequent generations, as was the case with Nzinga who continued the fight against the Portugese after her brothers passing.

RESISTANCE UPON THE HIGH SEAS

At every juncture, at all times throughout Europe's diabolical trans-Atlantic slave trade, resistance remained alive in the hearts and minds of the people. Even as the wretched slave ships crossed the high seas rebellion erupted onboard, a reminder that the people would not choose to remain captive. Revolts during such times weren't uncommon and certainly remained a measure to be employed at every given opportunity. Though history has failed to record every account of revolt, many accounts have been recorded to remind us of the valiant courage the people would exhibit, even against great odds, to recapture freedom.

There is the account of The Hope Rebellion ('Hope' being the absurd name of the wretched slave ship), where the kidnapped men were able to force their way on deck, killing crew members and taking charge of the ship. Such forms of resistance became, and remained, a necessary staple in the fight to regain freedom.

Consider, too, the Amistad Revolt of 1839, known as one of the most famous (recorded) revolts to have taken place at sea. The kidnapped men were able to seize control of the slave ship on the way from Cuba, slaughtering all but two slave traders who were then put to the task of steering the vessel back to Africa, the men subsequently regained their freedom. There is the 1841 account of the slave ship Creole, where the kidnapped men attacked the crew, massacred their enslavers, and set sail to the Bahama Islands, returning to freedom. Many examples fill the pages of history and bear witness to the measures employed by the people in resisting captivity and oppression. Such accounts also show that the vast majority of people did not resign themselves to captivity, oppression or slavery; nor did the people forfeit their inherent right to be free, unburdened by the diabolical whims of such systems.

RESISTANCE IN THE CARRIBEAN

"Do as the bull in the face of adversity; charge..."
--From "To the Persecuted" By Jose De Diego.

In October of 1492, all hell would break loose upon the indigenous populations occupying this Western hemisphere for thousands of years. As the pirate Cristóbal Colón (a.k.a. Christopher Columbus) sailed Queen Isabella's ships toward the Caribbean islands of the Atlantic Ocean, he would set off a process of destruction that has yet to be recovered from, even centuries later.

Seeking out gold for the Crown of Spain and wealth for himself and family, Columbus mistakenly stepped upon the lands of Caribbean Native Americans; this brought nothing but disease, destruction, and genocide. He set off a campaign that would eventually destroy lands, civilizations, cultures, people, peace, and freedoms that were enjoyed for millennia prior to his appearance. As Columbus illegally claimed the lands of the indigenous populations across the Caribbean islands, he would commence a series of excursions that would decimate the indigenous people henceforth. Columbus, due to massacring the people and conquering the land as he went, was always met with resistance.

Columbus encountered resistance for the first time in 1492, when natives armed with only bows and arrows successfully attacked his entourage as they attempted to navigate the island of Hispaniola (present-day Dominican Republic.) Moving on and sailing to the island of St. Croix, Columbus and his men were valiantly attacked by other groups of natives as they attempted to explore. Upon his return to Hispaniola in 1493, Columbus found his Fort (La Navidad) in ruins and his men dead, massacred on the orders of the local Chief Caonabo after their mistreatment of his people.

The native populations that Columbus would meet continuously resisted in the face of encroachment, and though they were oftentimes outgunned, the people remained persistent. At times, out of sheer hatred and frustration at their conditions, the people would destroy their own villages and fields retreating into the forests. In some instances, rebellion became so fierce that Columbus would resort to sending emissaries to meet with local Chiefs offering gifts, lies, and deceit in an attempt to forestall revolt. No matter the tactics employed by the natives, it was a constant reminder that resistance would not cease, regardless of the odds.

By 1495 a major revolt erupted, led by a coalition of local Chiefs on the island of Hispaniola in resistance to the colonist's brutal occupation of lands, plundering of riches, and rape of women. In 1502 the Higuey natives rebelled, seeking revenge for the killing of their Chief, a regular tactic the colonists used to subjugate the local tribal bands. Although many rebellions were put down, the spirit of resistance remained as the colonists continued to stretch their diabolical system across the islands.

Imperialism and colonialism would continue under

the rule of Juan Ponce De León, and by 1508 the system of the *encomienda* (in 1503, it was a system that granted a Spanish soldier or colonist a piece of land along with its native inhabitants) would have been, causing thousands of natives to be condemned to a system of organized slavery. Goldfields across the island of Puerto Rico would, by now, be buzzing with forced labor as enslaved natives were worked to death under conditions which nearly wiped out the entire population to the point of extinction.

RESISTANCE WITHIN MAINLAND NORTH AND SOUTH AMERICA

By 1513 Ponce De León had sailed and landed on the shores of Florida, beginning an exploration endeavor that saw Spanish explorers cruise along the northern shores of the Gulf Coast of Mexico, seeing Alabama, Mississippi, and Texas and thereafter sailing up the Atlantic coast to the Carolinas. By the time Spain reached mainland South America (Modern Mexico,) the ruler Moctezuma II was the most powerful and most famous emperor of his land. As the Spanish explorer Hernán Cortés landed on the Gulf Coast (Veracruz, Mexico,) he began a quest to subjugate the existing civilizations that spread across modern-day South America and declare himself its feudal lord. In his quest, Cortez would meet resistance at every turn. Shortly after Cortés infiltration into

Moctezuma's lands, he would meet up with Cuitlahuac (Moctezuma's brother) who forced the incoming Spaniards out of the area after fierce resistance, retaking the ancient city of Tenochtitlán. Along the central corridor of Mexico (present day Zacatecas,) the native Chichimecas Indians would engage in fierce resistance against Spanish encroachment that would go on for another fifty years.

Between 1539 and 1541, the Spanish explorers Hernando de Soto and Francisco Vásquez de Coronado had kicked off treks into the interior of North America, yet again introducing elements of disruption and destruction amongst the indigenous populations. Spain's thirst for gold, silver, and mineral wealth brought soldiers and missionaries into every corner of the continent. This led to hostilities, conflicts, and wars that would go on for centuries to come. As Coronado set out on his explorations, encroaching upon Pueblo Indian territory, he would meet resistance in the likes of the Pueblo warriors who eventually forced the Spanish to abandon New Mexico.

By 1680, the attempts to subjugate Pueblo territory was renewed, but resistance remained ever-present in the Pueblo warrior Pope, who would successfully force the Spanish out of Northern New Mexico after galvanizing and leading the people in armed rebellion. By the end of Spain's imperial/colonial bombardment within the Western hemisphere, three hundred years would have elapsed. These three hundred years would culminate with the devastation of cultures, near extinction of people, loss of original languages, and the loss of indigenous history and civilizations.

The price that human beings would pay under the imperial systems of the Spanish Crown's insidious plots of subjugation and domination should never be lost in the present. As we attempt to come to terms with the current condition of those who still suffer from the remnants of such systems, we must remain resolute in our understanding of the history which gave rise to our current condition. When we begin to lose sight of such history is when we begin to lose sight of the need to employ the types of resistance that the times we are living in may necessitate.

AFRICAN RESISTANCE IN A STRANGE LAND

"If there is no struggle, there is no progress.
Those who profess to favor freedom, and yet
deprecate agitation, are men who want crops
without plowing up the ground. They want rain
without the awful roar of its many waters. This
struggle may be a moral one; or it may be a
physical one; or it may be both moral and physical;
but it must be a struggle. Power concedes nothing
without a demand."

-- *Frederick Douglass*

By the early 1500's, Africans brought to the so-called

"New World" began to rebel and escape Spanish and Portuguese captivity. Joining the indigenous peoples, Africans began forming their own communities and settlements throughout the West Indies (and mainland America.) There began an amalgamation of people that would bring about new societies, and consequently, new forms of resistance. The amalgamations and new bonds that were forming amongst fellow oppressed people proved to be a form of resistance in itself as the native populations were now becoming replenished despite the continued decimation.

Some of these new communities and societies were formed by the Maroons. Consisting of escaped African and Native captives, the Maroon (origins from the Spanish word 'cimarrón' meaning feral cattle or wild, unruly) people would stake out their own territories in the hills, mountains, and forests with an aim at increasing hostilities, raiding and pillaging plantations, and harassing the slave owners at every opportunity. Their resistance was a constant reminder of impending revolt.

By the 1600's, bands of Maroons stretched along coastal towns of South and Central America. The revolutionary Maroon Bayamo and his followers escaped captivity, founding villages of their own and carving out an existence independent of the slave master's society in Spanish-controlled Panama. Such men were monumental in inspiring the people across the different geographical areas to resist. His leadership symbolized the ever-present spirit of resistance when all else fails.

Resistance against the vicious sting of captivity and oppression would constantly spring up as the Spanish and Portuguese raced to subdue the lands of the Caribbean and mainland America. The Miskito Sambu formed in 1640, from the revolted captives of a Portuguese slave ship taken over off the coast of Honduras/Nicaragua. The Miskito Sambu thereafter formed communities and blended with the indigenous people over the next half-century, staking out their own destiny. Tales of their valiant revolt were spreading across the landscape, encouraging the people to resist by all means.

In the Caribbean, one of the most famous Maroon societies was formed in Jamaica as escaped African captives joined the native Taino Indians already living there. This set off decades of resistance, which led to the First Maroon War of 1731, and the subsequent Maroon War of 1795. In Brazil, the famous Palm Nation Maroon Society sprung up in the early 17th century. This was a population of 30,000 free people living independently, ruled by their own King and maintaining independent existence for almost a hundred years. Their resistance paved the way towards freedom and dignity. Although oppression pushed in from every side, the people flourished. Remnants of these communities and people still remain to this day as a testament to the centuries-old attempts to regain freedom and dignity, in spite of the odds.

History is replete with accounts of the people's will to resist throughout the nearly seven-hundred-year period of slavery, destruction, and oppression let loose by Europe upon Africa, Native America, and their children. Perhaps the most famous and greatest act of resistance within the Western hemisphere came about in the Haitian Revolution of 1791. The revolution began with the resistance of Francois Mackandal, who led rebellions against plantation owners in Haiti for six years prior to the full-scale revolution that would go down as the most successful slave rebellion in history. It began as a revolt and ended with the founding of an independent state.

The rebellion persisted until 1794, when slavery was officially abolished in all territories and the famed General Toussaint L'ouverture established himself as Governor of the island. As Napoleon Bonaparte's armies attempted to reinstate slavery, General L'ouverture kicked off a full-scale revolution. By 1803 the French were completely defeated, and the people declared their independence and established the island as the New Republic of Haiti. The Haitian Revolution becoming a shining example of resistance and a pivotal point in encouraging others suffering under slavery in the western hemisphere to rethink their plight and utilize resistance in regaining those basic human rights owed to each member of the human family.

Toussaint L'ouverture's revolution would send

shockwaves across the oceans into mainland America. The news of what began as a slave revolt culminating into full-scale revolution and the establishment of a free black state would cause concern amongst the perpetrators of slavery throughout the Western hemisphere. Simply put, the enslaved and oppressed peoples from all corners of the continent and the Caribbean islands would now gain inspiration through the example of the resistance displayed by the valiant people on the island of Haiti.

NATIVE AMERICAN RESISTANCE IN NORTH AMERICA

"Brother, when you first came to this Island you were as children, in need of food and shelter, and we, a great and mighty nation. But we took you by the hand and we planted you and watered you and you grew to be a great Oak, we a mere sapling in comparison. Now we are the children (in need of food and shelter)."
--(Opening speech often used by Northeastern Indian Leaders at conferences with Europeans during the colonial period)

The original people inhabiting the Americas have, in their story, many told and untold realities of slavery and oppression which brought about centuries of resistance in the face of deceit and colonialism. As the pilgrims set foot on their lands, the natives would nurse them back to life only to be later rewarded with treachery and disease. Native Americans experienced high mortality rates. The biggest killers were smallpox, measles, influenza, whooping cough, diphtheria, typhus, bubonic plague, cholera, and scarlet fever. All imported by the Europeans colonists.

With their lands stolen and many lives lost the natives would be forced into hostilities, leading to famine and wars that would become the norm for a people who had previously lived in harmony with the land, animals, and nature for millennia.

The English began to settle on the lands of the Pamunkey Indians by 1607 in North America. Exploration of land and natural resources would drive the colonists to heap atrocities so great upon the people, that the remnants of such would be visible to this very day. Every tribe and nation of Native American Indian would come to taste the poison of the English. Disease would begin to ravage tribes along the coastline from Massachusetts to Maine, leaving a trail of death that the native had never known before. By the 1620's, the relationship between the Euro-colonists and natives would grow hostile. War would break out between the two, causing the English Crown to settle in, employing violence against the people until populations began to dwindle significantly. Their eyes set upon the most fruitful pieces of land to be inhabited; the colonists stayed a course of devastation that can still be witnessed today, half a millennium later.

Over time, forced onto land and territory unsuitable for their sustenance and survival, the tribes and nations of natives would suffer for years to come. As the Euro-settlers began to arrive in droves, colonizing every corner of the land, devastation would become a prominent fixture. In the southern parts of the land the attempt to institute slavery upon the natives would be initiated by the Euro-colonists. The native Cusabo, Westo, and Choctaw tribes in the Deep South were all harassed as attempts to enslave them became frequent. After years of migrations, a result of Euro encroachment and invasion, the native people were eventually, and permanently, displaced. Reservations were set up, forced movement was employed, and land thievery became the normal ploys and tactics of the Euro-colonist/invader.

As the warrior spirit of the Native American would have it, resistance would emerge as the people continuously attempted to regroup. By 1675 the native revolutionary Metacom, with a significant following of Abenaki, Nipmuck, Narragansett, and Wampanoag Indians, would attack more than half of the ninety English settlements in New England. Further south, the resistance of the Susquehannock Indians in Virginia raged on as the people refused to give up their land. As the displacement and reshuffling of the people became widespread, the tribes and nations began to band together, establishing treaties amongst each other in opposition to colonial encroachment. The Pueblo revolts took place out West as the Spanish were forced out of native lands by the hostile Tewa, Tano, Picuris, Taos, Jemez, Acoma, and Hopi. These tribes would all put up valiant resistance, fighting intermittent wars for as long as they were able. The constant warfare and skirmishes, fought as a result of the colonial attempt to subdue the native people, would amount to a massive decline in the Native American population all over the continent. This resulted in Euro-colonists illegally confiscating millions of acres of land from the native people.

From the early 1700's to the 1850's, in the eastern parts of North America the resistance of the Black Native Seminoles of Florida would join forces in resisting aggression and encroachment. Runaway slaves from the southern parts of the east coast would make their way to join forces with the native Seminole tribes. They eventually fought three major wars against European settlers. The Black and Native Seminoles became known as fierce warriors in the face of European attempts to unlawfully obtain their lands.

Resistance was always the first reactionary measure for these communities as the people continuously engaged in guerilla warfare against Euro aggression, never willing to accept oppression, slavery, nor the thievery of their lands. These wars would persist for years, going down as some of the fiercest conflicts ever fought between the United States and Native Americans.

Throughout the years of warfare and resistance, many native revolutionaries would emerge on the scene. As the territories become littered with Euro-colonists, vying for position over native lands, resistance remained ever-present. Militant and revolutionary prophets sprang up, prophesying that the European invaders would have to be driven out and off the continent in order for the native people to return to the customs of their ancestors.

One such persona was the revolutionary Pontiac, who would mobilize warriors from many different nations to strike at the English by any and all means. Pontiac's call to resistance led to the establishment of the confederacy of the Ottawa, Lenape, Wyandotte, Seneca, Potawatomi, Kickapoo, Shawnee, and Miami tribes. Together they initiated a short war against the British in an effort to push the Euro-colonists off native lands. At this juncture, over a hundred years had passed since the native people welcomed the Pilgrims on to their land as a gesture of good faith. Within this same period of time, the cultures and peoples of the Americas had been nearly wiped out by the Euro-onslaught.

By the 1800's the revolutionary warriors Tecumseh and Tenskwatawa began to rally the people toward resistance to stand against the United States, gathering thousands of fighters and warriors from amongst a diverse selection of tribes, forming a pan-Indian confederacy that was both political and military. Through these actions, the native people gained some of their lands as the European powers agreed to terms conceding certain areas back into native possession.

Decades of war and resistance continued. The War of 1812, The Creek Wars, The Seminole Wars, and The

Black Hawk Wars took place within the span of several decades in the 1800's. This was a testament to the peoples' never-ending desire to be free, unburdened by the whims of oppression.

Revolution and uprising will remain as long as mankind inhabits this earth. Taking the era of the Native Americans as an example, it is shown yet again that people will not resign themselves to slavery or oppression without employing resistance. Oppression summons resistance. The various forms of resistance largely depend upon the circumstances facing the people. The end result in the face of any form of oppression is always resistance!

RESISTANCE AMONGST ENSLAVED BLACK PEOPLE OF AFRICAN DESCENT

"Blacks know that there were millions of Americans who spoke about "freedom" and "liberty" for centuries without once thinking about Black freedom and liberty. They know as a deep lesson of history, that their ancestors were dragged here in shackles by people who swore that they were doing it "for their own good." They know from bitter experience that while Americans may say one thing, they mean something quite different. They know this."

-- *Mumia Abu-Jamal;*
Writing on the Wall

In the United States of America resistance brewed for centuries amongst the enslaved and oppressed. Revolts were common as slave owners were constantly tested by the spirit residing within all oppressed people to resist the brutality. The first recorded slave revolt in the United States happened in Gloucester, Virginia. A revolt that included white indentured servants as well as black slaves. The first all-black slave revolt occurred in Virginia in 1687. Prior to this date the only recorded reports of agitation were of black slaves forming groups intended on raiding and harassing slave-owners at any chance. Subsequently, and as history would have it, resistance would become the norm amongst those suffering under the heat of the diabolical system of slavery. The 1739 Stono Rebellion showcased the organized desire and determination of the people to escape slavery, during which the American south (Charleston, South Carolina) would experience one of the bloodiest slave rebellions in recorded history. The rebellion began as slaves acquired weapons and supplies. They embarked on a journey to the slavery-free, Spanish-ruled territory of Florida in a desperate attempt to gain freedom. Fighting against major odds, the rebellion inspired many along the way to join the resistance, rather than remain in the misery of slavery.

We find in America's ugly history of slavery the German Coast Uprising of 1811, known as one of the largest slave revolts ever recorded in terms of the number of people involved. Taking place along the Mississippi River, enslaved blacks planned to destroy sugar cane plantations, free fellow slaves in the State, and take control of New Orleans. Though outnumbered and limited in resources, the people pressed forward, taking up arms and inspiring others as they went about destroying plantations and displaying their desire to escape slavery and oppression no matter the cost.

In the chronicles of resistance against slavery, we find the story of Denmark Vesey in Charleston, South Carolina who would attempt to orchestrate rebellion using the ideals of the Haitian Revolution. These ideals spoke of the possibility that freedom would ultimately be obtained through the persistent employment of resistance. Vesey went to his death with these revolutionary words: "[the] work of insurrection would go on whether with or without [him]." Men and women such as Vesey remain in the history books as a testament to the never-ending desire of the people to resist and sacrifice in the pursuit of freedom even where death was imminent.

Perhaps the most well-known slave revolt in American history is Nat Turner's in Virginia. Turner's revolt would shake slave owners to the core, pushing them to prepare for war as Turner and the people went about wreaking havoc upon the lives of their oppressors. The revolutionary Turner began enlisting the help of other men to assist in the revolt and to put his plans into action. Though ill-equipped and unable to complete the ultimate goal of his vision, the sheer desire to resist and take back freedom was far greater than the reality of the odds stacked against them.

The valiance exhibited in the lives of individuals such as Denmark Vesey, Nat Turner, and others such as Harriet Tubman, Sojourner Truth, Marcus Garvey, Malcolm X, and Martin Luther King, Jr., to name a few, speak of an eternal partnership with the desire to be free and a willingness to challenge the odds in an attempt to reach loftier heights of freedom.

The history of resistance has provided valiant and unfathomable acts employed by those who suffered slavery and oppression. As we are reminded of the tragic but true stories of those such as Margaret Garner, who, under the immense pressure of slavery, would choose to kill her own two-year-old daughter rather than return her into the hands of slave-catchers to once again live a life of slavery and servitude, we are then able to take a glimpse into a life that was unimaginable.

Resistance against the diabolical system of chattel slavery was never modified to placate the expectations of the moral sensibilities of humanity. We must therefore ask ourselves: what type of slavery and oppression would mandate a serene form of resistance? The stark reality of escaping oppression is that the sheer desire to be free demands a multitude of measures in order for that the ultimate goal to be achieved. Resistance, in any form, must be employed.

As we begin to examine for ourselves the historical underpinnings covered within this chapter, we then begin to understand the physical as well as the mental anguish generations of innocent human beings were burdened with as a result of being forced into a life of abject torture, cruelty, oppression, and slavery on a daily basis that passed over a course of centuries. If now we fail to consider the reality created by the evil systems of imperialism, colonialism, and slavery we would be failing to understand the gravity of our present condition and dilemma in which we still find ourselves. When we lose sight of the realities associated with slavery, oppression, and their generational effects, we are blinded to the realities of these systems that surreptitiously lurk in our society.

***

THE INHERITORS OF RESISTANCE

"The use of language of slavery in any variation always strikes an exposed nerve in the United States. The result of guilt, denial and deep-rooted anger and frustration over the inescapable reality that our country's foundations are buried in the fields of slave plantations."
---William C. Rhoden, Author
"Forty Million Dollar Slaves"

In the past, many Americans have "fought the good fight" so that "We the People" might stand as a united body in resistance to those ideals which give cause to hatred and strife in our nation. Today the era of Donald J. Trump has caused Americans, of all backgrounds, to experience the heat of hate and racism (even though, personally, he may not display such traits.) Ideals in which the majority of Americans repudiate and have vowed to exterminate.

Although racists, bigots, and white supremacists have attempted to utilize "the Trump Era" as the catalyst in turning back the hands of time, we are also fortunate to be living in an era in which the vast majority of Americans, taking a page from their history (America's history belongs to all Americans,) are standing (or kneeling) in opposition to those ideals of intolerance, racism, hate, oppression, inequality, and injustice. As these concepts have no room to exist in America, the majority of the people have mobilized and are therefore utilizing a new form of resistance.

The present American generation must endure as we taste the bitterness of struggle that many freedom fighters in the past have tasted over the centuries. In tasting this bitterness, we will come to cherish the sweetness of the ideals which truly define America. As we observe from all walks of American lives from a wide assortment of backgrounds, a concerted effort to make a difference for the better in our society, we can rest assured that America's diversity is at work, countering the vestiges of hate and oppression that fester in our society.

Today, we witness as our parents and grandparents witnessed before us, a multi-cast of protests, movements, marches, and voices erupt all across America in opposition to inequality, injustice, discrimination, and prejudice. Whether the causes are women's rights and equality, L.G.B.T.Q rights and equality, movements such as #BLACKLIVESMATTER, #METOO or the like, the people are exercising their powers to effectuate change in our society. We are assured that resistance is abounding as the people remain involved and engaged.

***

In the past, resistance was not always an armed, physical affair but nevertheless persisted in the face of tyranny, slavery, and oppression. Over the centuries, resistance has taken on many forms. Plots, escapes, revolts, insurrections, revolutions, protests, and marches have filled the pages of America's history beginning with Europe's inception of its diabolical slave trade within the Eastern and Western hemispheres. From a line of freedom fighters stretching throughout the centuries up until the modern Civil Rights Movements to the present-day protest, the people have stayed a steady course in resisting oppression. The very souls of the people speak of struggle and resistance, and whether expressed in their music, art, fashion, dress, language, folk lore or traditional stories, their lives are consumed by this.

The brief historical events presented to the reader in this chapter were presented in an attempt to substantiate the premise of Colin Kaepernick's protest. Some may ask the significance of highlighting slavery and oppression as juxtaposed against Kaepernick's protest? The short answer can be found in the historical underpinnings that give rise to the current black and brown dilemma prevalent in our society. When we consider such a past we then realize that Kaepernick's stance was not taken in a vacuum, but in opposition to those permeating vestigial remnants of slavery and oppression that today parade under the guises of "Police brutality, mass incarceration, racial profiling, education inequality, "economic inequality, inadequate health care, employment inequality, unemployment, discrimination and a plethora of ills that disproportionately affect black and brown people in America at alarming rates. Under these conditions resistance will continue, and though some may detest the people's pursuit of true equality and "Justice for All" the quest will continue. For this reason, we can thank Colin Kaepernick for his iconic sacrifice

CHAPTER 3

Systemic Oppression

"If equality is granted in the area of education; it is denied in housing opportunity. If it is granted in the health care services, it is denied in terms of father's income level. If it is granted by law (Brown 1954), it is denied through social practices etc."
-Francis Cress Welsing

Oppression - n.1. The exercise of authority or power in a burdensome, cruel, or unjust manner. 2. An act or instance oppressing. 3. The state of being oppressed. 4. The feeling of being heavily burdened, mentally or physically by troubles, adverse conditions, anxiety, etc.

I must first lay the premise as to why I chose to undertake the task of gathering like-minded individuals to help bring forth this work. My duty is to help those who are blind to see, those who are deaf to hear, and those who are ignorant to understand the reality of life for people of color. I've watched critics disparage Kaepernick's protest (kneeling) despite his reasons. Kaepernick has given multiple statements as to why he is protesting during the national anthem: he was kneeling for social injustice, inequality, and the way America oppresses black and brown people.

I felt I would be doing this book a disservice by not highlighting the ways in which minorities, mainly black and brown, are systemically oppressed in the United States and under their flag. It's no coincidence that Kaepernick can no longer sit back and do nothing as media outlets repeatedly show unarmed black men, women, and children killed, murdered, and gunned down and not feel a connection. I don't expect everyone to understand what such a connection feels like. For me, I see my father, my uncle, brother, cousin, son, nephew or friend. These are the reasons people of color protest and rebel against an establishment that is supposed to protect and serve the people. Assata Shakur once said: "People get used to anything, the less you think about your oppression, the more your tolerance for it grows. After a while people just think oppression is the normal state of things. But to become free, you have to be acutely aware of being a slave."

Some people simply remain "asleep." As Dr. Francis Cress Welsing pointed out in "The Isis Papers:" "Oppression is forced submission and cooperation in any of the areas of labor, law, politics, religion, and/or war." Therefore, oppression comes in a variety of forms here are just a few: blacks live six years less than whites. Black women live on average four years less than white women. The infant mortality rates are two times higher for black babies than they are for white babies.

Discrimination is discrimination no matter your social

class, tax bracket, position or title. When people of color leave the lower class and join the middle or upper class they are perceived as better, but one thing never changes: skin color/race. The ills plaguing people of color do not change as they move on to a higher class bracket, middle class whites still live ten times longer than middle class blacks, economic discrimination still plagues blacks and they are still considered less qualified in the job field than their white counterparts, simply because of color. In health care, discrimination remains a hurdle. The service that health care providers and hospitals offer depends on multiple factors including skin color, insurance, and financial capabilities all of which keep black and brown people at the bottom rung of the healthcare debacle. There are people being turned away because they don't have the insurance or funds to pay for medical bills. Hospitals fall under the category of public service and no one should undergo mistreatment or be turned away based upon status (status is determined by color/race.) There are patients dying in America as they wait on the lines of "red-tape" and "bureaucracy." They lack the funds, which is compounded by discrimination (which in turn causes them to suffer the higher rates of health-related sicknesses and maladies on a generational scale,) black and brown people continuously lag behind in the area of health and fitness. It's just another effect of systemic oppression.

As black and brown people remain behind in society,

the biggest gap can be found in education. Though it has been sixty years since the passing of <u>Brown vs. The Board of Education</u>, the school system is still separate and not equal. Was Brown supposed to be our road to an equal educational system? Then what happened? As young children begin their education, disparities have been shown in terms of the learning gaps that exist between black and white children. It has nothing to do with their ability, but rather the proper exposure. Black children lack skills such as color identification, math, matching shapes, and vocabulary. Maybe this can be attributed to black families having less access to educational material due to economic struggles? Or could it be the lack of enthusiastic educators, who feel the need to strike because they can barely sustain themselves and their own children and families on their little-to-nothing salaries? Or is it that educators cannot teach (especially in public schools that already operate on limited budgets) because funds are not available to purchase textbooks and other vital educational materials?

Black children are more likely to be enrolled in low-quality daycare, and are less comfortable reading due to the lack of education. The current standard school textbook doesn't appeal to and is excluding the black adolescent because of the lack of diversity. Retention rates (for children of color) are astronomical, although holding students back proves no benefit academically or socially. Black students make up only around 16% of school enrollment but account for 32% of students who receive in-school suspensions, 42% of students who receive multiple out-of-school suspensions, and 34% of students who are expelled. Black children are arrested more and are referred to law enforcement more often than their counterparts.

There is a lack of diversity within the school system, which in turn results in these alarming statistics. Students are more likely to respond to staff that look like them or those who show serious compassion. The lack of diversity in public schools causes you to pause. White principals make up 80% of the public-school system. Only 6.2% of high school teachers across all subjects are black. The school system needs to take into consideration the environmental issues that affect a child. Teachers and staff are sometimes perplexed as to why these children fall behind in class or have behavioral problems. Black children have the greatest rate of any race for families living in homeless shelters. Nearly 25% of black parents report their children live in unsafe neighborhoods, compared with 7% of white parents.

Growing up "black and poor" can have some pretty serious effects on a child. Black children are more likely to have emotionally traumatic experiences marring their childhood such as abuse or neglect, the death or neglect of a parent or witnessing domestic violence. The maltreatment of children is 14.2 per 1,000 for blacks and 8 per 1,000 for whites. Most black high school students admit they have been raped. Black youth at all levels are more likely to be victims of violent crimes. I know these statistics may not mean anything to some, but when a child or parent is faced with uncertainty in regards to food, shelter or clothing it makes growth difficult. Families living in poverty experience abuse at higher rates and live in environments where they witness gruesome crimes on a regular basis. So the last thing on a child's mind is school work. When you look closely, it's easy to see how systemic oppression affects people of color.

***

"It must be realized that the mass incarceration of blacks, specifically black males, ultimately contributes substantially to black genocide, as it takes black males to make black babies and ensure future generations."
-Dr. Francis Cress Welsing

The number one constraint placed on black minorities is the criminal justice system. Taking a black man out of the household plays a vital role in the destruction of successful parenting. However, the effects can far exceed any prison sentence. Due to the rules as dictated by welfare, if a person has a criminal record then he is automatically barred from living in that household and an individual is subject to lose their benefits if such a violation is found to exist. As of 2016, 39.7% of Non-Hispanic Blacks were in receipt of some form of welfare assistance. This inevitably poses an issue for a recently released felon attempting to re-build their life given the limitations imposed on them in terms of where they are able to reside, resulting in a financial chokehold. A hypothetical yet very real scenario, what does a father do when he is the sole provider for his family and is unlawfully harassed, discriminated against, and arrested for a simple traffic ticket or some false charge? This father is forced to make an almost impossible choice; pay his ticket (which will take food out of his family's mouths) or fail to pay the ticket and feed his family. It would seem that the father is doomed regardless of what choice he makes. If he fails to pay the ticket then he will be charged a late fee, which can ultimately land him in jail, resulting in his family having to find a way to financially support themselves. Or he can pay the ticket and watch his family go hungry. Either way, unpaid bills will no doubt pile up leading to him and his family being thrown out on the streets. There is no happy ending to this story. Often these real issues of financial chokeholds can result in poverty for the family or worse, a combination of poverty and the father's incarceration. Mass incarceration does not just affect the individual whilst in prison. Once they are released, the retribution continues as their right to vote is often withheld completely or for a specific time period. This prevents them from electing officials who hold powerful roles within law enforcement, judiciary roles, and lawyers. This leaves a felon stuck in a perpetual cycle of constraints specifically designed to keep them powerless.

For black and brown people in America a chokehold, although deemed as excessive force, is often used in an attempt to physically force compliance and co-operation. There is, however, a metaphorical chokehold which is used to prevent progression and development of black and brown people. A chokehold is a restriction used to coerce submission. A chokehold adds pressure to the body for noncompliance. A chokehold is intended to bring a subject under control, either causing pain or placing them in an unconscious state. Such examples of metaphorical chokeholds are mass incarceration, stop and frisk, voting rights, war on drugs, and all other discriminatory practices. The stigma is to blame African-Americans for their own demise, over 100 years after slavery. Blacks are still exploited and continue to deal with some of the same plagues, if not more. These modern constraints reduce the competition for jobs by economic standings, for the most part, in favor of white Americans.

Examples of such are in law enforcement and corrections. Most prisons are built in rural areas and the cash flow of these institutions are handed to the white working class. Blacks have a second-class citizenship because more often than not, despite having the same qualifications and similar in relation to age, education, marital status, etc. as their white counterpart, when being interviewed for jobs there is still a significant lack of diversity. One has to look no further than the Tech Industry or any Fortune 500 company. This is especially true when it comes to black women. Being part of a disadvantaged group, coupled with a minor criminal record and now you're "X'ed out" of the competitive work pool. Simply put, you have been systemically disqualified from the process, another symbolic chokehold.

This is why we need more people of color in congress, in boardrooms or even courtrooms, not only when laws and rules are being put in place that can directly affect people of color from moving forward but also so our value can be properly displayed and our interest properly protected. The criminal justice system needs to be reviewed, as Jim Crow practices are still very much alive and well. The blame extends throughout the entire system: from the judges who hand out disproportionate sentences to black men and women, to the prosecutors who recommend these sentences, to the judge with no remorse from the public defenders, and lawyers who are merely there to push the defendant through the criminal justice system as if on an assembly line, to the politicians who care more about their political gains, and lawmakers who work more so for lobbyists than for the people. This does not imply that everyone who commits a crime should be released, but there are so many innocent victims in prison as well, including those with sentences that do not fit their crime. Therefore, the system is "broken by design."

*THERE ARE MORE AFRICAN AMERICANS IN THE
U.S. CRIMINAL JUSTICE SYSTEM THAN THERE WERE
SLAVES IN 1850!*

***

It would be a disservice to this writing if it did not
highlight the ways in which minorities, mainly black and
brown, are systemically oppressed in the United States,
how systemic oppression follows a child from birth to
adulthood. It's a never-ending cycle. Rapper "Jeezy"
coined the phrase: "Don't get caught!" Don't get caught
in a system that is systemically targeting and
perpetuating bias against people of color as they continue
to constrain and navigate our ambitions through specific
mediums. For example, in Eldridge Cleaver's book, *Soul
on Ice*, he stated: "by crushing leaders, while inflating the
images of uncle toms and celebrities from the apolitical
world of sport and play, the mass media were able to
channel and control the aspirations and goals of the black
masses". Though there is nothing wrong with being an
entertainer nor a celebrity, one has to only look at the
television and see the parade of commercials praising
black entertainers and athletes (especially during Black
History Month,) and the popularity and rewards they
receive to understand that our masses will see those

deliberate images and admire those persons and professions. This sways us from aspiring to be doctors, lawyers, engineers, scientists or work in other fields of expertise needed in our communities. This is mainly because there is no glory shown in these professions their importance is not on our radar, so to speak. This is, as Eldridge Clever explained to us, a "form of control." However, it is not the system's tactics that should be feared the most here, but the fact that the majority of my people, including myself, do not fully comprehend what is at work.

If we can use these same mediums (i.e. television, media outlets, and other powerful institutions) that are usually used against people of color to our advantage then we are on our way to creating an offensive attack on systemic oppression. This tactic has been revealed to us by Kaepernick's stance; by effectively using the NFL's platform to gain the attention of the media, to create social awareness, and a social movement.

CHAPTER 4

Original Intent

"Here, equal justice under the law is prescribed only for the
corporate rich and powerful. There are literally thousands of people
imprisoned solely because of their race and poverty."
Benjamin F. Chavis Jr., 1978

"Land of the free:" this is part of the American national anthem; however, it has become more and more apparent that this only applies if you are white and have a certain level of financial freedom. Considering the continuity of making such a bold claim ("Land of the Free,") America is acknowledged as being the world leader in the incarceration of its people. With only 5% of the world's population, they proudly boast 25% of its inmates. In the 1980's and 1990's, their "tough on crime" politics fueled an influx in the country's rates of incarceration. At the end of 2010, there were 1,267,000 people in state prisons, 744,500 in local jails, and 216,900 in federal facilities: a total of more than 2.2 million prisoners. 60% percent of those locked in cages are people of color. Realistically, black males in their twenties risk a 1 in 3 chance of being locked up. Currently, three-quarters of the prison population who have been convicted of a drug related offense are people of color. "Nationally, approximately 5.3 million Americans are denied the right to vote because of laws that prohibit voting by people with felony convictions. Felony disenfranchisement has resulted in an estimated 13% percent of black men being unable to vote." (American Friends Service Committee: 2013.) Mass incarceration adversely affects black and brown communities and their families. It reinforces societal stereotypes of black/brown men and further fuels the single mother pandemic. It also continues the cycle of oppression of the black/brown communities as children are left without male role models. Effective rehabilitation does not exist within the American justice system and therefore reoffending (recidivism) is consistently rising. Add to this a lack of voting rights for felons, and the black/brown community is held in a perpetual and consistent state of modern-day slavery "The power of the ballot we need in sheer defense, else what shall save us from a second slavery?" (W.E.B. DuBois.)

Mass incarceration is an extremely profitable business. The idea that prisons are a means of keeping society safe has long been forgotten and has now been replaced with the need to earn (prison Industrial Complex) offensively large amounts of money for the individuals and corporations who were assigned the task of running these privatized systems of caging human beings, "The Bureau of Prisons paid $639 million to private prisons in the fiscal year 2014, averaging $22,159 per prisoner. For perspective, that's about the same amount it would cost to send three people to a state college." (Jenn Rose, 2016:1)

The private prison industry is a booming business and it makes financial sense for everyone involved to keep an ever-increasing prison population on the rise. 19% of federal prisoners are incarcerated in private prisons, and 6.8% of state prisoners. This presents a captive market in terms of profits for companies that are offering services within the private prisons. For example, telephone companies are often unregulated and can set their own level of charges, which can result in phone calls costing as much as $15. The companies who provide commissary are able to sell their goods at a cost five times the normal retail price, enabling both companies to make an estimated profit of 1.2 billion dollars and 1.6 billion dollars, respectively. This system is set up in such a way as to promote profit for the companies and financially vested individuals, and yet promote institutionalization for the prisoners. In this system a person is left little to no choice but to conform wholeheartedly to the restraints of captivity and inevitably. This leads to the dehumanization of prisoners, a lack of autonomy, and eventually the inability to cope with the demands of real life upon release. They struggle to make autonomous choices with regards to daily living and become embroiled in the continuous cycle of reoffending and stuck in the cycle of the criminal justice system.

The ridiculous and lengthy sentences that are given to people who commit crime are also questionable, not to mention the criminal justice system's institutionalized racism. Consider this scenario: a black/brown male returning to court to fight an already outrageous life sentence. After the court case, the life sentence is withdrawn but the presiding judge (federal) hands down an equally ridiculous sentence of 101 years. Any sane person can see this as unreasonable. It is unimaginable that such a lengthy sentence can be seen as justice. This undoubtedly feeds into the annihilation of the black/brown family, subjugation of the black/brown man, and this amounts to an implicit, covert effort towards the continuous devastation of the black/brown segments of this society. As society continually has to endure the monetary cost of this system, the concept of rehabilitation and freedom becomes secondary. "The cost of liberty is less than the price of repression," (W.E.B. DuBois.) Yet somehow, the American people habitually endure and accept this ongoing oppression.

To understand how racially biased the system is, we can compare the current "opioid epidemic" to the past "crack epidemic" because opioids are affecting suburban whites in those areas of society that are considered "white," the handling of the "epidemic" is geared towards rehabilitation rather than incarceration, as was the strategy used to combat the "crack epidemic." The reason for the difference in "tactics" is simply based upon the difference in "who" is being affected and who society deems worthy of imprisonment (black and brown people.)

This is a perfect example of how a system that was never designed to protect black and brown people or work for black and brown people operates within a society ruled by white privilege.

The historian Ira Berlin, made the distinction between "slave societies" and "societies with slaves." The north of America was made up of cities that had slaves which defined it is as a "society with slaves," whereas the south was a "slave society" because its political and economic infrastructure was solely dependent on slavery. When slaves won their freedom, the economic stability of the south crumbled. It was imperative to rebuild their economic infrastructure and as is stated in Ava DuVernay's documentary "13th," the 13th Amendment inadvertently assisted in this rebuilding of the economy by vilifying and criminalizing black people. The 13th Amendment made it unlawful to enslave another human except if they had committed a crime, beginning of mass incarceration and the denigration of black people in general, but more specifically black males. This produced a new slave labor that was adhering to the confines and restrictions of a constitutional law. Being released from slavery with absolutely nothing, then forced into an era of segregation which relished in the continued existence of oppression and socio-economic deprivation of black and brown communities only resulted in an increase in poor housing, poor educational opportunities, poor employment prospects, lack of healthcare, and deprived living conditions. "Poverty is the worst form of violence," (Mahatma Gandhi.)

It was no surprise that when drugs exploded on the scene, black and brown communities resorted to either selling drugs as a way of improving their financial situation or using drugs as a means of escape. Violence and drugs work hand-in-hand. If you degrade, oppress, denigrate, and destroy a people long enough eventually they become the very thing society has portrayed them to be. With the 1990's "War on Drugs" and the 1994 bill that introduced mandatory sentences, three strikes rules, and no parole (in federal system) the country without a doubt worked towards the utter destruction of the black/brown family, continued the cycle of poverty, violence, and oppression of black/brown people but specifically the black/brown male. When you consider that 1 in 17 white men will face incarceration during their lifetime as opposed to 1 in 3 black men, it becomes apparent that the system is racially biased towards black/brown people.

If you commit a crime, your punishment is to serve your time within the confines of prison, then re-enter society and begin to rebuild your life. In America, once you are convicted of a felony you no longer have the right to vote, which currently is an estimated 6.1 million Americans, you will inevitably struggle to find employment and face a myriad of other such suffocating restrictions that reduce or in some cases diminish all opportunities for progression to a brighter future. For 1 in 3 black/brown men, it is reminiscent of the segregation era when black people were refused the right to vote or gain adequate employment. Currently, black men account for 6.5% of the U.S. population, but a staggering 40.2% of the prison population. There are more men incarcerated now in 2018 then there were slaves in the 1800's. The latest phenomenon is the rate of black women being incarcerated. "From 1977 to 2011, the number of people in state and federal women's prisons increased by 600 percent from 15,118 to 111,387 ("Understanding Mass Incarceration," James Kilgore.) Kilgore noted in reference to the incarceration rates of black women that "Black female populations nationally declined more than 30 percent during the first decade of the twenty-first century. Despite this decrease, black women still maintained by far the highest per capita incarceration rates, nearly three times that of whites and almost double that of Hispanics." Black women had previously been left to bear the burden of the single-family household and are now being removed from that role, thus the entire family structure is destroyed and the black child is left to fend for themselves, ensuring a generational cycle of the "pipeline to prison."

97% percent of the people behind bars have never been to trial. The poor are, more often than not, unable to afford bail and with the use of coercion and scare tactics which appear to have become the norm in America, it is understandable that most prefer to accept a plea deal than face court and a possible minimum mandatory sentence. This can be a ridiculous amount of years in prison. For some, this also means accepting a plea deal despite extensive evidence proving their innocence or at the very least casting doubt on their guilt. Take the case of Kalief Browder's ordeal with the system for example. He was adamant that he had not stolen a backpack; therefore, he refused a plea deal. His family were unable to afford the bail money ($10,000) and he was then held for three years in Rikers Island where he suffered torment and abuse at the hands of both prisoners and guards. Two years after the charges were dropped and he was released, he took his own life as a direct result of the abuse he endured and his subsequent solitary confinement. These things combined induced his mental health issues. So many innocent people are incarcerated despite evidence to prove their innocence because it would seem the American justice system lacks justice.

Prison reform will never occur as prison is too lucrative a business for all involved. For reform to ensue, it would mean that the constant stream of prisoners would dwindle. It would also equate to an admission of wrongdoing on the part of the past and present governments, judges, prosecutors, and anyone else responsible for mass incarceration. "You must be the change you want to see in the world" and sadly white history and white privilege cannot allow that admission of guilt to ever be verbalized, therefore change will be almost impossible to achieve (Mahatma Gandhi.) America continues to incarcerate those we believe we can oppress with little or no recourse: black people, brown people, and other poor people within our society. "You can judge a society by how well it treats its prisoners," (Fyodor Dostoevsky.)

With the invention of for-profit prisons, there are two major companies that run these establishments. GEO and Corrections Corporation of America (CCA,) both have channeled more than 10 million dollars to political candidates since 1989, and have spent an astounding 25 million dollars on lobbying. A prime example of someone who has used his political prowess to profit from private prisons is Marco Rubio (Republican) who used his influence to secure a 110 million-dollar contract for GEO and has also accepted large financial donations for campaigns. This has an adverse effect on disenfranchised people within the country. For example, this privatization enabled a cash scandal, where two judges in the state of Pennsylvania received payouts from for-profit juvenile facilities to increase the number of adolescents to these centers for extended periods of time.

It breeds an environment similar to slavery in that humans are traded openly in return for monetary gain, at the expense of the most vulnerable amongst us: children, immigrants, and the poor. "This is America," (Rap Artist: Childish Gambino.)

Judiciary bias exists and has been widely acknowledged by black people and people of color who have had first-hand experience of this, but with the emergence of present-day movements and their promotion on social media, the world is becoming aware of white police, judges, and lawyers inability to empathize with or see potential in young black and brown men. Two 17-year-old men both robbed corner stores in Florida same crime, same circumstances yet the outcome of their sentences were worlds apart. Both 17, both charged with armed robbery, both from the same county in Florida, both with juvenile records, both offered plea bargains. With all the same factors involved, common sense would tell you they received the same sentence, but that was not the case. One of these young men was white and was given 6 years of probation, the other young man was black and given 4 years in prison. This is not the only case of injustice. A lack of understanding between cultures is often used to explain such disparities in sentencing but is this really a viable reason or is it merely that young black men in particular, are not seen as having potential and a racially unjust system fails to empathize but rather judges and condemns because of their inherent blackness. If you do not believe this to be true then you are part of the problem as opposed to being an active member of the solution. Whether a young black man commits a crime or is the victim of a crime, Trayvon Martin, Michael Brown, (the list is endless) the negative language used to depict their character is criminal and racially coded to enable us (society) to be accepting of their fate. For example, Trayvon Martin was not seen as the victim but rather the media focused on the fact that he had been suspended from school on three separate occasions as if this was proof he was criminal enough to warrant the sad and brutal end of his life by a sick vigilante. Alternatively, a young white man who commits a heinous crime is labelled "troubled, geeky, shy" in a purposeful manner in order to evoke empathy. For this reason, Kaepernick insists on equality of the races, which is not meant to insinuate we demonize white young men, rather we empathize with all young men regardless of race and surely in 2018 this should occur without question, but instead only white people are afforded the same.

CHAPTER 5

Both Sides of the Coin

"There is no doubt that if young white people were incarcerated at the same rate as young black people the issue would be a national emergency."
--Dr. Cornel West, Forward, The New Jim Crow

White Privilege

It seems as if many white people do not understand or fail to admit that they benefit from an invisible backpack full of white privilege. Though poor whites can be subjected to some of the same systemic issues geared towards people of color such as gentrification, poor schooling, poor health care, etc., the difference is when you're white in this society and you 'clean yourself up' you are then liable to be rewarded with that backpack full of white privilege. For those who beg to differ, here are some statistics that may provide some clarity: today blacks earn less per hour (men 22%, women 34%) than white men with the same education, experience, marital status, and region of residence according to Economy Policy Institute. You may still say: "opportunities are available" and "you can be anything you want to be," but in reality society can't help but look at people of color as inferior descendants of slaves. These popular phrases are thrown around without considering the realistic consequences of systemic injustice, and these phrases become just sound-bites of the so-called American Dream. How can I or anyone of color have the same degree as our white counterpart and earn a similar salary? It is largely based on the color of my skin. Again, white privilege. Inequality is one of the issues that forced Kaepernick to muster the courage to kneel and therefore garner massive support. Census statistics indicate that the annual median household income for blacks is $35,544 compared to $55,775 of the rest of the country. More than 25% of the black population lives below the poverty line, while the national average is 14.7%. Though you see minorities graduating at higher rates, the unemployment rate remains at record lows and the stock market is continuing to break record highs. The question must be asked: who is actually benefiting from all of the nation's success in the economy? These improvements continue to fail in narrowing the equality gap and the inclusion of diverse groups of people. It would be a false pretense to surmise that black America is on the rise.

The Federal Reserve reported: The share of Americans' income was held by the top 1% of households which reached 24% in 2016, a record high and the medium net worth of white households at $171,000. This number was nearly 10 times larger than black American households. Those findings show us that even though our economy continues to excel in many areas, it's not a reflection of society as a whole. The America that is portrayed is more of a dream than a reality, as the wealthy benefit the most. In laymen terms the gap between the "have's and have not's" has not narrowed, as blacks and Hispanics are continuing to fall further and further behind. One in five blacks are serving virtual life sentences in America's prison warehouses and seventy percent of minority children are born out of wedlock. There are multiple factors, such as the broken family structure that stems from mass incarceration and black fathers being the biggest population affected.

These conditions do not assist in building positive atmospheres for children to be nourished. Blacks receive significantly higher sentences than their white counterparts, why is that? We assert that the reason is to destroy the head of the family (the black man) and aid in destroying the unity of the black family. There is a stigma attached to black males in this police state we call America: aggressive criminal or thug. Being treated as such leads to being pulled over, harassed, abused, disrespected or profiled for the type of vehicle we may be driving. There are instances where the neighborhood in which you live or you may visit subjects you to traffic stops, searches or even illegal arrest. There are those blatant bigoted instances reminiscent of the days of segregation, where if you have a white counterpart in your vehicle you would be subjected to discriminatory violence or even death.

Today driving while black is a real charge, sometimes leading to arrest or death. It happens whether you're in a predominantly black or white neighborhood. These problems are not experienced by white people that is white privilege. Black privilege is... Eric Garner being choked to death by police officers after being accused of selling cigarettes; Trayvon Martin being shot and killed by a neighborhood vigilante for wearing a hoodie, but how does wearing a hoodie make you a suspect? Philando Castile being murdered by police in front of his fiancé and child on Facebook live for the world to see and no one questions the purpose of the traffic stop to begin with; Michael Brown being murdered for raising his hands equates to why his hands weren't raised high enough; Walter Scott running away with his back turned and being gunned down by a police officer and critics questioning why he ran; Freddie Gray handcuffed, dragged, and beaten to death as police officers have charges dropped and acquitted. Sandra Bland's family was offered a $1.9 million settlement despite claiming she "committed suicide" in police custody; Stephen Clark being shot 22 times and officers silencing body cams, and the defense was he had something shiny (a gun.) In every instance the defense is "I was in fear for my life," well the man had a cellphone. This is what "black privilege" looks like. Parents are thankful that their family members make it through another day (at the writing of this book, these scenarios will not have ceased.) I can remember around the ages of 16-22 when I was under my mother's roof. She would constantly call and check on me. Many times I ignored her calls but now I truly understand her worries, back then I was insensitive to her concerns. These are the same concerns that black and brown mothers all across America are facing. Even after being presented with these statistics and facts, some will still say "there is no white privilege" or ask: "what is white privilege?"

A recent online video went viral of a college professor conducting an exercise with his students on the school field. They were going to have a race; the winner would get $100. For the students who were athletically gifted, they were in for a rude awakening. The race was setup to mirror real life. The students assembled on the goal line. As they began, he instructed the students to take two steps forward if these questions or statements applied to them. If the statements had no bearing, they were to stay where they were.

He began: "Take two steps forward if both of your parents are still married."

"Take two steps forward if you grew up with a father in the home."

Some students moved forward while others remained.

"Take two steps forward if you had access to private education."

"Take two steps forward if you had access to a free

tutor growing up."

"Take two steps forward if you never had to worry about your cell phone being shut off."

Very soon, the students where spread out across the field. Some ahead, others behind, and some still at the goal line.

"Take two steps forward if you've never had to help your mom and dad with bills."

"Take two steps forward if it wasn't because of your athletic ability you don't have to pay for college."

"Take two steps forward if you never wondered where your next meal was going to come from."

Just before the race was about to begin, the Professor asked everyone near the front to look back.

"Every statement I've made had nothing to do with anything any of you have done, has nothing to do with decisions you've made. You still got to run your race but whoever wins this $100 dollars, I think it would be extremely foolish of you to not utilize that and learn more about someone else's story." Just as life goes on, so did the race. After the race ended, the teacher added "If you didn't learn anything from this activity, you're a fool." Now that's what I call white privilege and a large part of the reasons blacks are so affected as a direct result of systemic oppression. This is what our brother Colin Kaepernick is kneeling in silent protest for; he wants equality and justice for all, and not just white individuals.

***

"When you're fighting for justice and democracy; color, race,
and social class have little importance…
Man taken in his totality transcends questions of race."
--Jean-Bertrand Aristide

White Allies

A white ally is exactly what the term denotes; a white person who is an ally to the cause for justice and equality (though opposed by some whites) by showing their allegiance through deeds and action. They are willing to lend their hand and voice when it appears that a black person (or a person of any other race) is voiceless or is being oppressed.

One such "ally" is Jane Elliot, a former teacher, anti-racism activist, and educator as well as a feminist and an LGBT activist. Jane Elliot gained notoriety for her "blue-eyes brown-eyes" exercise, conducted for her class the day after Dr. Martin Luther King Jr., was assassinated and a student asked: "why they shot that King?" To better her student's understanding of the discrimination that lead to Dr. King's assassination she utilized the difference in eye color, instead of the difference in race. Though not many people across the nation agreed with her "experiment" (lesson) with race, she endured the ridicule and scorn in the face of hate and continued to promote awareness in regard to the issue of race discrimination that was prevalent in the United States at the time.

***

In 1963, white supporters and activists in the fight for justice and equality in America were labeled "Nigger Lovers" by their fellow whites for joining the Civil Rights movement, and although they faced backlash, harsh treatment, threats on their lives, and in some cases even death, these individuals persisted in the fight. These allies have a legacy going back to white abolitionists such as Lewis Tappan, one of New York City's most prominent abolitionist who put his spirit, energy, and wealth into the Anti-Slavery movement, he actively assisted fugitive slaves seeking freedom. The story of folks such as Grace Anna Lewis, a member of the rural Quaker families that assisted fugitive slaves who passed through southeastern Pennsylvania during times when even the laws prohibited assisting fellow human beings seek out freedom and dignity. These are the footsteps that "white allies" follow when they disregard hate's status quo.

"There comes a time when silence is betrayal," (Dr. Martin Luther King Jr.) This means white people are faced with the conundrum of how best to support their fellow black citizens (or any other oppressed group). In the fight for justice and equality, white people must adhere to their inner strengths and determination when challenged by the existing evils of racism and discrimination.

The stories of our "white allies" should inspire us, as it is imperative that allies track the history that underscores the push for freedom and equality in America. Allies such as Passmore Williamson, Thomas Garrett, James Miller, and Robert Purvis dedicated long periods of their lives as activists in the attempt to free those held captive under the abominable system of slavery. These men understood the push for the freedom of a particular people is ultimately a push for the freedom of people as a whole.

Silence in the fight for freedom, justice, and equality is unacceptable for those of us who profess these same ideals. At times silence is either the fear of repercussion for outward support of the fight towards equality, lack of knowledge on how to show unwavering support or merely being content with the current status quo. As we acquaint ourselves with allies such as Maria Weston Chapman, we begin to understand what it takes to break down these illusionary barriers that may be causing us to "cheer from the sidelines." Maria Weston Chapman used her inherited wealth and began what became known as the National Anti-Slavery Bazaar held annually in Boston in the mid-1850's, and attracted thousands of visitors. Though the premise of the Bazaar was to advance the goals of the Underground Railroad, it also became influential in harnessing female domestic skills and offered a platform for female activism in the fields of business, commercial, and public affairs. Though faced with opposition and challenges from the prevailing gender norms and other controversies, Maria Weston Chapman's works continued and the success of the underground railroad continued to flourish because of white allies such as her and many others.

***

Just as in the past, white allies must not only push for change but also remain visible to black (and oppressed) people across America and worldwide, clearly demonstrating that the issues are not just a very real concern for black people alone, but the issue of racism is something so evil and oppressive that even white Americans harbor a strong desire and need for it to be eradicated. The importance of white allies is born out of the real need for unification on both sides. These images are what so many of the past (and present) sacrificed for.

Today, there are many examples of white allies who encourage us to stand united in the face of divisiveness and intolerance. These individuals support not only fair treatment of their fellow black and brown citizens, but also the dismantling of the systemic racism that we face in the workplace. An example can be found in the words and actions of the San Antonio Spurs coach, Greg Popovich, a person who has never minced his words when speaking on topics related to race and equality. Recently, "Coach Pop" stated, "The league is made up of a lot of black guys. To honor (Black History Month) and understand it is pretty simplistic... How would you ignore that? But more importantly, we live in a racist country that hasn't figured it out yet. And it's always important to bring attention to it, even if it angers some people. The point is that you have to keep it in front of everybody's nose so that they understand it, that it still hasn't been taken care of, and we have a lot of work to do." His words clearly demonstrate that racism and intolerance should be confronted, regardless of who may feel uneasy or uncomfortable.

How inspiring is it when the average American can look towards prominent individuals of our society and see that the responsibility to confront injustice and inequality is not lifted according to status, wealth or race? This is why allies' such as the Golden State Warriors coach, Steve Kerr's voice becomes so important on issues that affect not only his players, but people in society as a whole. Coach Kerr has been outspoken on social issues on several occasions and has not hesitated to defend his players when they stand against racism and injustice. When his team decided to decline an invitation to the "Trump White House," coach Kerr promptly accepted the team's decision, and joined them in solidarity. When his team decided to enjoy something more fulfilling than placating to the ego of president

Trump, he joined his team and 40 kids from the D.C. area on a tour of the Smithsonian Museum of African American History and Culture in the nation's capital.

Steve Kerr explained his experience in these words: "If you've never been before you have to go, it's one of the most powerful experiences you'll ever have... The way the Museum is designed is beautiful. It goes from despair and hopelessness at the beginning of the African slave trade. You're at the bottom of the slave ship, you read about the history. It's just devastating, and you wonder about the human spirit and you wonder about the people, are they good or are they evil? All these existential questions go through your mind, and as you go up, each level, there's more and more hope and you have more and more faith in the human spirit and you're amazed at the resilience. How would any of us respond in similar circumstances? And yet you get to the top level where there's this amazing cultural excellence in the African American community through sports, history, politics, medicine, music..." These are the experiences that bring people together and these are the experiences that white allies must continue to share with society in an attempt to influence others who eschew hatred and injustice and who seek out examples on how to express their sentiments in a society (or personal environment) that may scrutinize and ostracize them for daring to have a voice.

***

Sports in America has always been one of the unifying factors when we are faced with adversity and strife in our society. Through sports, individuals are exposed to other people and situations that normally they would have never encountered. In these cases, we are able to see the true spirit of individuals as the shackles of ignorance or tribalism are removed and replaced with empathy and brotherhood. Through this occurrence, allies are formed.

For a modern-day example, Philadelphia Eagles player Chris Long (who happens to be white) supported his teammate Malcolm Jenkins (who happens to be black.) Long had no problem supporting his brother when he chose to raise his fist during the national anthem in support of Kaepernick's silent protest. The imagery of Long's support of his brother and friend was, and is, enough to inspire us who find it hard to escape the confines of the box society people we know may attempt to place us in. There are young people (as well as old) who will see those visual images of support and ultimately mimic what they see.

On a more personal note, Long wasn't just looking for visuals or to be looked upon as an ally, when he joined the conversation by placing his arm around his brother in solidarity. His act spoke volumes and allowed us to have a glimpse at what it means to exemplify decency and compassion in our daily affairs, even when some are being "rubbed the wrong way." Chris Long shows his allegiance not just in actions but in deeds as well. In 2017, he donated his entire base salary ($1 million dollars) to benefit educational charities. The Chris Long Foundation will donate his next 10 game checks to organizations that support education equality in the three cities that he spent his 10-year career playing in Philadelphia (Eagles,) Boston (Patriots,) and St. Louis (Rams.) The campaign "Pledge 10 for Tomorrow" encourages fans and businesses to donate or match his contributions. Chris Long never publicized his donations, but eventually decided to do so after the negative outcry surrounding the national anthem protest and the unfortunate violence during a Ku Klux Klan rally in Charlottesville, VA that led to the unfortunate death of a young woman counter-protesting racism.

Throughout the "Anthem melee," questions have been asked in regard to what these socially active players were doing with respect to individual endeavors that could count towards effectuating change. Long felt compelled to share what his contributions to the social-ills plaguing our society were, and when questioned gave this response: "The scholarships were going to happen anyway. But I think to do it publicly, is kind of turning a negative into a positive. There are a lot of positives. We want to promote diversity and equality and educational opportunities. That's something I've been passionate about for a couple of years." This is not just an ally speaking, but a human being with a heart.

The reality is that individuals such as Long exist in every corner of our society, but if we remain silent, society will be deprived of these blessings. Long continues to push education reform. His teammate and brother, Malcolm Jenkins, continues to push criminal justice reform and despite their different agendas, they are staunch in their support for one another. What will we do as allies? Pushing forward in all positive agendas pushes our nation forward. As a people, as a nation, and as one we must remain united.

***

There are those sad and unfortunate times when an ally pays the ultimate price so that we (the people) enjoy the fruit of their labor. Pain morphs into joy when we understand that the universe sends us (the physical world,) those souls whose purpose in life is fulfilled when inequality is destroyed in their name or as a result of their presence on earth. One such beautiful soul was given to us in the name and form of Heather Heyer, a young ally whose life was taken by hateful, racist, white supremacists as she stood peacefully promoting justice on behalf of her fellow citizens. She was a true American, she embodied the spirit of America.

Though we never heard her voice, she spoke to us

through her sacrifice. Her death cannot and will not be in vain. The spirit embodied in her is the spirit that will "make America great again." "In estimating greatness, one should consider the intensity, sincerity, and capability which an individual plays [his or her] role, whether that role is large or small. To exclude a great 'small' man because his life gave him a small role and include one whom it appointed to play a larger role seems to me to be idealizing the stage and not the individual," (J.A. Rogers.)

The principles Heather Heyer engendered were exemplified in the simple act of attending a rally; her attendance gave the world an insight into the spirit residing within her. A spirit of a true ally in the fight against racism, hatred, and bigotry. Heather's role in life was a great one, and her life will always be associated with the fight for tolerance, equality, and justice. She gave us the ultimate sacrifice as a testament to the innermost character of her soul... she will forever be an ally.

CHAPTER 6

Spiritual Death

"But Jesus said unto him follow me; and let the dead bury their dead"

Matt 8:22

The above scripture verse carries more than just a religious connotation, it is taught by life itself that a physically dead person cannot bury another physically dead person. Here, it is obvious that Jesus is referring to the "spiritually (mentally) dead" individual. Today, our communities are collapsing into a spiritually dead state. The question must be asked, however, by what means are our communities so rapidly becoming spiritually dead? I contend that the oppressive socio-environmental conditions perpetuated upon most of the poor and uneducated by the "power structure" produce, in effect, a state of helplessness which if left unattended sets the stage for spiritual death (mental hopelessness.)

The most common, but illogical response to impede this severe mental state is to simply hope that such oppressive conditions change themselves with time, but as Huey P. Newton once said: "We hope for change without really thinking what the odds are of such change just happening." We must face the realization that nothing would actually change (for the better) unless a behavioral strategy is developed and carried out to change our collective condition. I do not speak of picking up "The Good Book," parading one's self into some institution, and "laying your burdens down" as this is not a behavioral strategy, but merely another unconscious attempt at fending off the suffocating weight of spiritual death, in common practice by most elders of our communities.

Our youth moves toward a more destructive, but equally useless refuge: drug dealing. The "inner-city" youth quickly realizes that they are constantly surrounded by a spiritually dead community. Because the youth are not or have not yet been politically educated they cannot draw the line from their inherited condition and state of existence to the "power structure" that administers government. Therefore, our youth incorrectly assumes that the lack of capital is the root cause of their community's piss-poor conditions. So in a vain, misguided, and ignorant attempt to not befall the same fate of mental hopelessness they witness on a daily basis, most of these youngsters pedal the only successful commodity in close proximity: dope. However, their faulty logic is unsuccessful as it does not cease the unyielding blows of oppression. Instead it merely increases the stress level in these young adults, as the "projects" (containment centers) in which they live are already targeted for incarceration. Their induced participation in this fixed game of drug dealing just makes them even more visible to self-justifying "enforcement officials" that are trained and ordered to harass, terrorize, brutalize, and murder... with impunity.

However, there is yet another futile escape: the club scene. If one is conscious enough and willing to pay close attention, particularly to the "night life," then all would agree that when times are at their worst, when they present themselves to be the darkest, the club scene flourishes. We leave the ghetto in back to back cars like a funeral procession on our way to the club. Why is this? The answer is simple: the club scene is just another weapon used by the unfortunate against despair. The club is where party goers seek to dance themselves into fatigue, relieving the pent-up anxiety, stress, and frustration of the day, week or even month to the rhythm of the music. These practices, as pointed out by Francis Cress Welsing, in "The Isis Papers," prevents problem solution:

"Patterns of behavior that can be described as inducing semi-trance states, such as rhythmic hand clapping, singing, dancing, excessive rock music playing, listening to radio music, and shouting in religious settings... these practices of course avoid problem confrontation and thereby prevent problem solution"

Problem avoidance using dance can be said to be group specific as it traces back to Pre-Algerian Revolution:

"Another aspect of the colonized affectivity can be seen when it is drained of energy by the ecstasy of dance. Any study of the colonial world therefore must include an understanding of the phenomena of dance and possession. The colonized way of relaxing is precisely this muscular orgy during which the most brutal aggressiveness and impulsive violence are channeled, transformed, and spirited away. The dance circle is a permissive circle. It protects and empowers. At a fixed time and a fixed place, and under the solemn gaze of the tribe, they launch themselves into a seemingly disarticulated but in fact extremely ritualized, pantomime where the exorcism, liberation, and expression of a community is grandiosely and spontaneously played out through shaking of the head and back and forward thrusts of the body. Everything is permitted in the circle".

-Frantz Fanon, The Wretched of the Earth

It would seem that music and dance are our primary way of problem avoidance. For example, according to Mr. Brookshire Harris, in his book *Billionaire Branding*, he states that the creation of Rap music emerged within the black community as:

"An outlet for frustrated youth to overcome trials and tribulations of living in poverty and surviving in a system that they felt was ignoring their plight."

True enough, there are individuals that do not fall within the categories mentioned above and do not have similar ways of dealing with systemic oppression. These individuals are usually people that engage in or display misdirected aggression. These individuals do not find comfort in ball games or social events. They still must, consciously or unconsciously, alleviate their suppressed anger and pent-up hostility of negative emotions brought on by daily encounters with his environment's oppressive conditions. These individuals are the ones seen unleashing violence on their own communities as: "this repressed rage, never managing to explode goes around in circles and wreaks havoc on the oppressed themselves. In order to rid themselves of it they end up massacring each other, tribes battle on against the other since they cannot confront the real enemy," (Frantz Fanon.) These are the brothers in desperate need of guidance, and our communities are in desperate need of them. For they are the ones that need to be organized to defend us against the outside physical forces that threaten our very existence.

There are those that I have been hesitant to mention. For example, those that incorrectly assume that government assistance programs are of benefit. Indeed, government assistance can be helpful to some under certain circumstances, but it should only be utilized for a limited time. The constant reliance upon government assistance helps more to diminish its beneficiary's self-respect, work ethic, and self-sufficiency. As Sojourner Truth expressed to the newly freed men about the assistance from the Freedmen Bureau: If they were to continue taking government assistance they would in turn lose their will to work. To a certain extent, that is exactly what is happening to some in these days and times. It is only a matter of time, in these situations, before spiritual death sets in.

In the last analysis these sometimes-lucrative coping mechanisms are but temporary "release valves" to avoid the necessity of facing and fixing the elusive problem of oppression; and no amount of Sunday sermons, dope peddling, MC-ing or partying can defeat the impending "spiritual death" that looms like shadows over a candle-lit room.

It must be acknowledged that regardless of how fruitless these practices usually are, one must still bear in mind that they are still, a form of rebellion. Dwelling within this seemingly hopeless mental state resides the existence of the dogged strength and potential to regain mental resurrection. We need only to rediscover what is needed to initiate the process.

Kaepernick's protest has given momentum to a much-needed conversation in communities being viciously strangled by the ills his protest is premised upon. Kaepernick's highlighting of the atrocities that plague and continue to weaken this great nation is without doubt a part of an initiating process. This process should invigorate as well as inspire people into self-analysis, group discussion, and ultimately group mobilization; which "introduces into each man's consciousness the ideas of a common cause," (Frantz Fanon.)

Kaepernick's stance has revealed and put forth our common cause, while sacrificing his career. In him we have found an uncompromising figure/leader, one that must be praised but also one whose example we must have the courage to follow. We would be remised if we failed to utilize the current momentum in acknowledging and pursuing our collective responsibilities to reverse this infectious mental condition; a condition that has been latched on to by the unfortunate. We must now identify these areas of shortcomings for what they really are and rectify them. We must also begin isolating tactics employed for oppressive purposes by systematic forces. Remember, our mental resurrection cannot occur unless we are all actively engaged in making our physical surroundings conducive for such resurrection to take place.

CHAPTER 7

Preconceived Notions

"Your perception is not my reality..."
Actual Facts.

Society has preconceived ideas, which began during slavery, of what it means to be a black man or woman. The black man is only good for breeding, crime, selling drugs, and incarceration whilst the black woman is independent, uneducated, and the only thing she has to offer is sex. "...black women were deemed to be governed by their libidos and portrayed as Jezebel character[s]...in every way the counter-image of the mid-nineteenth century ideal of the Victorian lady," (Wikipedia, 2017:6.) The black woman's image is still tarnished by stereotypes forged by white society; it becomes imperative for us as a people to eradicate such degrading beliefs by not allowing ourselves to become self-fulfilling prophecies, but rather fighting against those negative images. "You know, it's not the world that was my oppressor, because what the world does to you, if the world does it to you long enough and effectively enough, you begin to do to yourself," (James A. Baldwin, 1973.)

Our ancestors did not fight for the right to be free and educated so that we could throw it away and become who others perceive us to be. Our women are more than their sex and sexuality, a woman should strive to achieve more than being someone's "baby momma" and objectified. Women should strive to exemplify the queen that she is. Whilst the black man should no longer be happy to live a life dedicated to crime, drugs, lack of education, and using his ability to procreate as a means of demonstrating his manhood. Men should strive to be the king that he is. Our environment may be a product of how societies dictate we should live, but that does not mean we have to adhere to being a product of our environment.

***

When Barack Obama was sworn into office, I like so many others, watched in amazement and hoped this might be the change we needed. Despite our hopes, little improved for us. In fact, they seemed to spiral out of control for the black community, more specifically for black males. The first time I heard of Kaepernick's silent protest, I couldn't understand why it caused such a negative response when clearly it was an emotional, personal, and well-thought-out reactionary display of support and outrage, caused by a spate of unnecessary murders of unarmed black men and boys at the hands of the people who supposedly "serve and protect" us. As a black man, Kaepernick made a conscious decision to use his professional, public platform to exercise his right to voice his outrage and show solidarity to the very people who were suffering. I can only assume that it was no longer an option for him to sit back and silently observe these atrocities.

All too often we vocalize our outrage in the safety of our own homes, but never take the steps to formalize a public reaction and attempt to redress the balance of inequality. The outright murder of black men is not unusual as it has occurred countless times in both England and America, but it was apparent that the numbers were increasing and it was all because someone could be demonized simply by the color of their skin. What further enraged our communities was having to watch the police officers responsible for the unnecessary use of force and these senseless murders, allowed to walk away from criminal accountability, unscathed by their actions.

As I continued to watch this singular man use his platform to garner more and more publicity for the injustices we were all privy to, it occurred to me that the people most vocal with regards to their interpretation of events were the very people who saw no wrong in a black life being blown out as easily as a burning candle. Their spin became his lack of allegiance to a great nation and his ruthless disregard for the bravery displayed by the military. This incongruent twist on reality made no sense in light of the outpouring of support via social media from veterans. However, the truth is that our military, past and present, are the very people who have throughout history willingly fought and, in some cases, paid the ultimate price to afford us freedom of speech.

***

I find it laughable that any protest by a minority ethnic person is portrayed as a clear display of disloyalty and non-allegiance to the flag and military. The reason these non-violent protests are immediately highlighted and discussed in such a negative fashion by the right-wing media and politicians is to appeal to the majority of patriotic Americans. Because of their innate need to silence the black community, it became increasingly important to garner support and the narrative needed to evoke sympathy from the people for their personal or political agenda. The best way to do this is to appeal to the country's patriotism.

Now, whether I agree with this extreme patriotism or not is irrelevant. However, I would have to question both the loyalty and allegiance that our countries have towards our soldiers. Many of us have family members who served, or have served, in the military. But what happens to these brave men and women once they have left the military, which they were so willing to give so many years of their lives to? The answer is very simple; they are discharged from their role with a simple yet friendly goodbye, nothing more and nothing less.

Transitioning to civilian life is extremely hard for most ex-military, add to that a physical disability or PTSD as a result of fighting in a war, and limited and inadequate support services, it isn't surprising that members of our military end up unemployed, homeless, suffering from mental health issues, having drug and alcohol issues, and in some cases committing crime and in the worst-case scenarios taking their own lives. The statistics are there, but where is our true patriotism when our military men and women are really in need? We are hypocritical when we claim they are being "disrespected" by those protesting injustice, when these protests also cover the injustices faced by our military men and women.

How patriotic are we towards these veterans and active members? If we are happy for them to serve and protect us, fight for our freedom of speech and against tyranny and oppression, but once they return home or are no longer active we would like nothing more than for them to integrate into society and do so quickly and quietly. Can we then claim that silent, powerful protests such as the #takeaknee protest is degrading, unpatriotic, disloyal, and demonstrating a lack of allegiance and support for our military yet on a grand scale we do the same on a daily basis? If taking a knee goes against our fundamental beliefs of how wonderful our troops are and how we should support them, surely our need to recognize their efforts should be demonstrated in how we treat them once they are integrated back into society, and not just leave them to fend for themselves without support.

It begs the question, how hypocritical are we? We are happy to declare our love and support, as long as it correlates to our argument and fits our purpose. In the United States and Britain, we celebrate Veterans Day (USA) and Remembrance Sunday (Britain) but we only remember or show thanks if and when it suits us. To combat and defeat Kaepernick's protest, it works for us to vilify his efforts. However, do we not ostracize and demoralize our servicemen and women every time we allow them to reintegrate into society without adequate resources? Is that not a similar form of oppression that the #takeaknee protest is battling against? During the outrage that many directed at Kaepernick, he made it abundantly clear that he would 'not stand for a flag that practiced oppression of black people and the oppression of black people within the military.'

In the United States, the suicide rate of deployed veterans currently stands at a staggering 41% higher than that of any ordinary citizen. This is indicative of our treatment of the men and women that serve in the military and the lack of adequate resources and support offered to them (we can also check the statistics on the acts of violence committed by ex-military based on their lack of resources and support after service is rendered or terminated.) This begs the question, as a person of color (or white service member,) why would you fight for a country that will not only abandon you once you have served your purpose, but also who doesn't respect you as an equal in terms of status after service? Do we then blame Kaepernick for openly stating "I am not going to stand up to show pride in a flag for a country that oppresses black people and people of color," letting the world know that "to me this is bigger than football and it would be selfish on my part to look the other way," (Colin Kaepernick, NFL Media, 2016.)

***

Kaepernick, like so many of us, has witnessed and experienced racism. He was privy to the senseless killings of black men within the United States and it became paramount that he voiced his opinion on that artificial reality created to feed an individual's personal or political agenda based on their over-inflated sense of importance. Like Kaepernick, the more we begin to live life and learn about real history, we then begin to see how racism and oppression has affected us as people—regardless of color—our cultures, family values, and ideals. As we educate ourselves it becomes gravely important to be aware and have a wider understanding of how racism, oppression, and slavery are still negatively impacting our societies to this day. It is apparent that this form of revelation is what drove Kaepernick to kneel for what is rightly expected in our society.

At the time Kaepernick decided to begin expressing his concern in regard to some of the ills plaguing black and brown people in America, 987 people were killed by lethal force at the hands of police. Of those murders 223 were black, a staggering 23%. This had become too much and resulted in his need to take a very public stance. There were a number of factors as to why he may have felt that he could use his platform to show solidarity to his fellow Americans, who so happen to be black and brown. We can assume that racism within America played an enormous role in his stance as there is no secret to its existence. When we witness the way black people are mistreated by police, it becomes impossible to deny that inherent and systemic racism plays a predominant role in these interactions.

Take this for an example of Kaepernick's outrage. Dylan Roof massacred nine innocent people during their bible study, he was arrested and quietly escorted to a police car, taken to get a burger to eat and then placed in jail. In comparison, Eric Garner was placed in a chokehold and subsequently killed for a minor infraction (peddling loose cigarettes was the claim.) Aside from their crimes, the biggest difference was their race and how they were demonized, or not, according to the color of their skin. This was a guiding force behind Kaepernick's reasoning for his protest.

***

Kaepernick, opted out of his contract but, in spite of his outstanding ability on the field, has not been hired by any football team. A clear demonstration of how racism has once again been used to disenfranchise yet another person of color, a dilemma that enforces the real need for change. Let's weigh this perspective, there are some NFL players who have been accused or found guilty of domestic violence, yet we continue to celebrate these men both for their athleticism and as role models, which means that we ignore or condone their behavior off the field for the sake of what they can do for our favorite teams on the field.

Are we "representing the flag" when we cheer for our team under such circumstances? Or are we justified in enjoying the game while our fellow citizens are crushed under the weight of injustice?

Regardless of Kaepernick's personal sacrifice in this situation, his protest and his subsequent treatment at the hands of the NFL has highlighted the issue of racism globally and for the first time in many, many years. This has given the rest of us (in sports, entertainment, and the "regular Jane and Joe") the strength, power, and ability to join the struggle and realize that we not only have a voice, but we have the freedom and ability to use it with pride and gusto. In today's era of internet and social media sites, we can join forces and spread our journeys and message all over the world. Imagine the impact of a global attempt to influence change from people that positively affect their societies through sports and entertainment. Take for example the brother in England, Akala, who has been involved in the struggle and has highlighted systemic racism in his country for years, publicly educating people about racism in the UK on a not-so-large platform, but nevertheless educating. Akala's impact on the black community in the UK is unquestionable. Could we imagine the networking of individuals such as Kaepernick or Akala and how their activism could join us together as a global force effecting change on a global scale? Few public figures are willing to take such a leap or to make public their protest, highlighting the issues of racism within our own countries or around the world, although it would be inspiring for our young people to see the strengthening image of people of color around the world to occur.

***

Individuals and organizations such as Back Lives Matter and Colin Kaepernick threaten the ideology of white supremacy, whether in the public, corporate, sports or entertainment domains. They threaten the right wing's need for power, their delusional idea of an inherent birthright of supremacy based solely on the color of their skin. Though the ideology of the right-wing, white supremacist, "the guilty," attempts to hide behind the scenes, these individuals and organizations expose their true intent at every opportunity because their delusional idea of an inherent birth right of supremacy based solely on the color of their skin continually drives them to attempt to achieve their goal. This is the "problem" they seem to have with taking a knee or expressing the worth of a black life in America. The "guilty" understand Kaepernick's protest has gained momentum and has the potential to be the start of real change. Change that will finally see equality not just on a small scale, but large enough to effect change within our economic, educational, and judiciary systems too. For this, we can only stand and salute Kaepernick.

CHAPTER 8

Triune Circumstances

"To hate someone, to discriminate against them and to attack them because of their racial characteristics is one of the most primitive, reactionary, ignorant ways of thinking that exists"
-Assata Shakur

Media

At the time of the Central Park Joggers case (1989,) another rape had occurred in New York. The victim was raped and thrown off a roof. However, there was little to no coverage of this in the media. Why? Simply put, it was because both the victim and perpetrator were of the same racial background. In the media the terminology used to describe the juveniles, in this case, were reminiscent of Emmett Till: the victim was white and the alleged attackers were black. So it was a media lynching using words such as wolf pack, beware, monsters, mutants, and sociopaths. Trump placed ads in three major newspapers calling for the return of the death penalty within the state of New York. He would not have called for the death penalty to be brought back had the young lady in the Central Park incident been black or Hispanic and raped by someone of the same racial background within an inner city in a socially and economically deprived area.

The mayor at the time, Edward Koch, said that this case would be a test to see if the criminal justice system worked. If this were to be a test of the system, it failed. It failed these five young black boys. From the lack of DNA evidence that would tie these boys to the crime, to the obviously coerced confessions, to the falsified and inaccurate timeline created by police to place these boys at the crime scene. All this case successfully proved was that as long as you were black, the system would be manipulated in an outrageous way to punish you for something you had absolutely no involvement in, with little to no consequences for those involved.

Culpability

In 1967, the Detroit Riots happened as a direct result of institutionalized racism as well. At the time it had been recorded that of the 93% of white police officers that worked for the Detroit police department, 43% of them were working in black neighborhoods but were deemed to be anti-black, and 34% were described as prejudiced.

During the riots, a number of people were held by police after an occupant at the Algiers Motel fired a starting pistol. During this ordeal the police officers, guardsmen, and state troopers beat, intimidated, humiliated, and abused the men and two white women they were supposedly "investigating." Also, during this time 3 of the "suspects," all of which were black men, were shot and killed. All three victims were unarmed. The officers involved were charged and faced court proceedings. The jury was made up of entirely white peers and as a result, all the culprits were acquitted of any wrongdoing. The victims in this event were not so easily let off as the repercussions of such a horrific ordeal left them scarred and traumatized. This was in 1967, at the height of the civil rights movement and yet the similarities between 1967 and 2017 are striking and scary. 50 years later racist, prejudiced, and trigger-happy police officers are still tried at the hands of a jury made up of predominantly white peers, the victims are always vilified and inevitably the police are acquitted of any wrongdoings or criminal charges.

In the United Kingdom, there are striking similarities. In 1966 there were suspicions of bullying, violence, and possible murder of a homeless black man at the hands of two white police officers. Although the officers were not charged with murder or "grievous bodily harm." Instead, they were found guilty of "actual bodily harm" and served a prison term for this. As a direct result of this horrific incident, the police started an organization called the 'Independent Police Complaints Commission' (IPCC,) which was created as an independent organization that would investigate any complaints against police or major incidents they were responsible for. The reality of this organization is more shocking when you delve into the members and their exact role. They are almost always ex-police officers that are in the IPCC and they have the power to determine whether or not police are charged or taken to court to answer for their supposed wrongdoings and sadly in the vast majority of these cases, the IPCC chooses not to prosecute the police officers involved.

So, it clearly demonstrates that in the United Kingdom our police are not answerable to the law either. This is not something that was limited to the UK's past, but more recently in 2017 a former Premier League soccer player was killed at the hands of police when unnecessary force was used and he was tased more than once, which resulted in Dalian Atkinson going into cardiac arrest and passing away. Clearly this is evidence of why we have organizations like "Black Lives Matter" and why Kaepernick began his silent protest and why he wore his now famous "pig socks" to clearly identify his displeasure and the displeasure of many others when police go bad or are unashamed of their outright disregard for the position they hold and the oath they took to serve and protect all. I can only imagine that Kaepernick had this deep-seated drive to openly share his inner disgust, hurt, and empathy toward victims and their families and rightly so. As Martin Luther King Jr. once said: "The ultimate measure of a man is not where he stands in moments of comfort and convenience, but where he stands at times of challenge and controversy."

Despite the personal and professional repercussions of his actions, Kaepernick could no longer sit by and accept the harsh reality of life in America for people of color. "People of Color have been targeted by police. So that's a large part of it and they're government officials. They are put in place by the government, so that's something this country has to change. There are things we can do to hold them more accountable. Make those standards higher. You have people that practice law and are lawyers and go to school for eight years, but can become a cop in six months and don't have to have the same amount of training as a cosmetologist." (Colin Kaepernick, 2016)

As Martin Luther King Jr. also said, "Our lives begin to end the day we become silent about things that matter," and clearly Kaepernick and a number of other individuals and organizations are not prepared for their lives to end because of their personal fear or inability to stand up against the injustices that occur every day in our so-called great nations. Real freedom can only exist without the presence of fear.

Vilification

There is more and more evidence that history is continuously repeating itself for a number of reasons

Firstly, and more importantly, we have experienced limited progression since the time of Martin Luther King, Jr. and Malcom X. Secondly, throughout history we are reminded at different junctures that we "should never forget" yet somehow, we conveniently forget as long as it serves the greater good. In terms of controlling black society, it is always necessary and convenient to forget their trials, tribulations, and hardships. Let us not forget that within days of giving his most famous "I have a dream" speech, Martin Luther King, Jr. was classified by the FBI as the most dangerous man in America. A disturbing reminder of how America vilifies black people who shed light on injustice. Kaepernick has been vilified and is now rendered unemployable by the NFL, despite his skills on the field.

Recently, it was documented that Donald Trump made several references to a number of countries that are home to black people. For example: Haiti and Africa. He was quoted as saying, "why are we having all these people, from shithole countries come here? Why not people from Norway?" (Trump, 2018.) Naturally, this angered a great deal of people, and rightly so. It was an example of racism at its finest, as it can be linked to the racist ideology that Nordic blonde-haired, blue-eyed people are deemed superior by white racists. Even more degrading and demoralizing is that it came from the leader of America. However, his views are not shared by most people living outside of America. Americans and

Norwegians alike responded with the question: "Why would we move to a country with a shithole president?" (Twitter, 2018.)

It begs the question as to why America, the proclaimed leader of the free world, can have a President (and I use that term lightly in reference to Trump) that is overtly racist, misogynistic, and unable to professionally lead. Yet the people of America, despite their collective outrage, are happy to sit and wait for his term to end naturally. This would be the perfect occasion for the majority of America to take charge and demand immediate and effective change. "Government is instituted for the common good; for the protection, safety, prosperity, and happiness of the people; and not for the profit, honor or private interest of any one man, family or class of men," (Massachusetts Constitution, 1780:2.)

If men such as Martin Luther King, Jr., Malcom X, and Colin Kaepernick can be vilified for their beliefs and actions to effect positive change then why is it an impossibility to vilify someone who not only holds racist beliefs but feels very comfortable openly verbalizing them to the world? Surely we the people have an opportunity to not only demand, but be granted the right to a better, more qualified, more positive, impartial leader who can work towards a brighter, egalitarian country that works to enhance the lives of all its people. "I have a dream that my four children will one day live in a nation where they will not be judged by the color of their skin but by the content of their character," (Martin Luther King Jr., 1963.) This would definitely "make America great again."

Does Trump's overtly racist comments and his eagerness to claim that many white supremacist protestors are "very nice people," not justify Kaepernick's protest? It is irrelevant how Mr. Trump feels towards Kaepernick and his protests and beliefs. What is offensive is his declaration of what is legitimate from what is not. His focus is to question someone's patriotism rather than explore and rectify the real issue of inequality. Surely, he is the one being unpatriotic to the flag and country, especially when we consider his views and alignment with white supremacists.

In regards to the appointment of Steve Bannon, well known for his outright racist beliefs, David Duke, a well-known, longtime white supremacist, said this: "This represents a turning point for the people of this country. We are determined to take our country back. We are going to fulfill the promise of Donald Trump. That's what we believe in, that's why we voted for Donald Trump. Because he said he's going to take our country back. That's what we gotta do," (David Duke, 2017.) Does the flag really represent all that Donald Trump appears to stand for and believe in? If so, then it would justify anyone's reasoning to protest, when we examine that a country built on immigrants is now being led by someone who believes equality is limited to those who look like him.

CHAPTER 9

What We Want

"We want an immediate end to police brutality and murder of Black people."

"We believe that we can end police brutality in our Black community by organizing Black self-defense groups that are dedicated to defending our Black community from racist police oppression and brutality."

<u>Black Panther's Party Ten Point Program (#7)</u>

As I have intently listened to conversations held by so many black people of today, it seems that many of us have our priorities misplaced. Too many of us find ourselves preoccupied with trying to find individual worth through the accumulation of material objects, confusing such gains with progress, while constantly overlooking our most needed position as "community leaders." We must come to understand that regardless of how many material possessions we temporarily sport or the wealth we acquire individually, we are all still in a collective struggle to survive our own destruction and mass incarceration. The miseducation of black youth and "justifiable homicide" all contribute in genocidal fashion to our collective demise.

When we, via Facebook live, saw the "enforcement

official's" encounter with Philando Castile, we must fully comprehend that it was not a routine traffic stop being shown to us, but instead we were witnessing a vicious murder of yet another brother from our family tree. Such a display of blatant murder by an enforcement official, against this brother of ours, should have sent lasting shock waves through our community's nervous system. This should've compelled us as a collective to institute a behavior strategy to safeguard ourselves, our progeny, and community against what can only be described as a domestic terror attack on black life. Unfortunately, the sad but unescapable truth of the matter is that such incidents have been so common throughout our American experience and so frequently displayed by institutions (mainstream media,) that a deep-seated fear has emerged within our communities. This leaves us paralyzed in regards to self-defense, as pointed out by H. Rap. Brown when he stated:

"A lot of people though, are afraid to defend their own lives. They're afraid to take a chance for their own liberation. But there's no other way to be free unless you put your life on the line."

Instead of finding our power and manhood instantaneously by being willing to make the ultimate sacrifice, for the preservation and benefit of the whole, we tend to always abandon that power in place of fear by rationalizing away these overt acts of terrorism and engaging in victim blaming.

No matter how vicious the murderous attack on those such as Eric Garner, Michael Brown, Sean Bell, Tamir Rice, Freddie Gray, Philando Castile, and countless others many have created one excuse after another to rationalize our community's continued loss of life. This is accomplished by, first and foremost, pretending that there were options that were readily available to them that would have saved their lives in what proved to be fatal encounters. If Eric Garner had only raised his hands higher and not been such a massive figure, or had Sandra Bland not been so "uppity," or only if Tamir Rice had looked his age while playing in a children's park, or suppose Freddie Gray had not run, then they all would still be right here with us today.

These fatal encounters were never within the victim's control, nor were they premised upon poor judgment or training on the part of enforcement officials. Rather, the deliberate use of fatal force was used for the primary purpose of maintaining effective control, hidden under the cloak of justifiable homicide.

Question this: how could Dillan Roof, who just murdered nine decent church folk in cold blood, be apprehended by enforcement officials without incident, even though he was clearly armed and dangerous? While Eric Garner, who was unarmed, posed no foreseeable threat, and was merely suspected of selling "loosies" meet his death upon arrest? The answer is elementary, the former is not among the targeted group. We must remain forever mindful that the police force that are roaming our communities finds its inception in slave patrols, which had the central objective of the preservation of the slavery system. "The model of law enforcement responsible for what we know as "police officers" – did not originate in ancient times nor during the medieval period. Instead, it was conceived by a British man named Sir Robert Peel in 1812. The United States first adopted the community policing model for the purposes of organizing "slave patrols." That is, the first implementation of Peel's community policing model did not happen until the days of slave revolts – Nat Turner and John Brown – when more and more human beings, kept in forced captivity and labor, took the risks to run away for the freedom of the Northern states," (Counter current news.) This once informal group commissioned itself with the duty of chasing down runaway slaves, enforcing segregation, violating legal rights, and squashing attempts of blacks to organize themselves for self-defense. This is in part the primary reason why people of color and law enforcement have a seemingly irreconcilable differences. America's enforcement officials have always been an oppressive force and chief visible threat to black existence in American society.

The continued use of fatal force on the part of this

government-sanctioned entity, called "police" or "law enforcement," is costly to the American judicial system, both locally and federally. However, since deadly force against blacks and other minorities has continued unabated, it must be perceived by the power structure as absolutely necessary. Furthermore, such social policy has unintended outcomes such as when an enraged black man, Micah Xavier Johnson, on July 7, 2016 out of apparent frustration over the police murders of Philando Castile and Alton Sterling, ambushed and killed five police officers in Dallas, Texas while injuring nine others; or when ten days later on July 17, 2016 Gavin Long armed himself then shot and killed three law enforcement officials in Baton Rouge, Louisiana. This was in response to the unyielding murderous rampage by enforcement officials against black life. Make no mistake, this is not the advocating of violence, as the belief is unchanged that:

"We aren't hungry for violence; we don't want violence. Violence is ugly. Guns are ugly. But we understand that there are two kinds of violence: the violence that is perpetrated against our people by the fascist aggression of the power structure; and self-defense, a form of violence used to defend ourselves from unjust violence that's inflicted upon us."

Bobby Seale; *Seize the Time*

Therefore, the use of self-defense in our communities,

against this seemingly violent entity (law enforcement) is not violence, but intelligence. However, in order to be effective, it must be organized and not the result of a spasm. This is essential because, as Amos Wilson pointed out in "Blueprint for Black Power:"

"Organization impose order and direction on otherwise random, relatively diffuse, unfocused or erratic phenomena in order to generate a focused concentrated form of power directed toward accomplishing particular goals."

Our goal here is safety. Sure enough, there will be some that take issue with the idea of a "uniformed rank" amongst the black collective to impede external attacks for the preservation of black life. But these people, I'm sure, have yet to devise a plan sufficient to neutralize, counteract or oppose the killing of unarmed black men, women, and children at the murderous hands of enforcement officials in these United States. There will also be some that put forth the position that: "not all cops are bad." This is absolutely true. However, black and brown Americans cannot depend solely on the good nature of the select few within law enforcement while the rest run rampant through our communities, brutalizing and taking our lives. And there must be a deep understanding that no one can blame us for taking such action, as history can attest to the fact that "at each phase of this long train of tyrannies we have conducted ourselves in a very meek and civil manner, with only polite please for justice and moderation, all to no avail. We have shown a noble indisposition to react with the passion that each new oppression engenders... we have petitioned for judicial redress. We have remonstrated, supplicated, demonstrated, and prostrated ourselves before the feet of our self-appointed administrators."

-George Jackson, *Soledad Brother*

At the end of the day we fail miserably in realizing one thing: we are at war. Economically, socially, educationally and, frankly, literally. At times "the only way you can get rid of war... is through the process of war." particularly when "war has been unjustly waged against us in our communities," (Huey P Newton.)

At the time this was written, 223 black Americans have been killed by police since Kaepernick fearlessly took a knee in protest of police brutality, racial injustice, and the murdering of blacks and other people of color. I contribute this largely to our failure to organize around strategy to sustain our lives at whatever cost. Therefore, we continuously witness increased officer-involved shootings of black and brown Americans, as we sit back and question why? Instead of saying: no more. The unanswered, dehumanizing, genocidal tactics of social control employed without a proper response, lowers group self-respect and heightens our sense of fear. When such occurrences are found to exist, we must then re-establish our weight as human beings by understanding that: "courage is not a talent but a choice." It's the difference between being completely swallowed alive by fear or saying goodbye to convenience. In the poetic words of Claude McKay:

"If we must die, let it not be like Hogs Hunted and penned in an inglorious spot, while round us bark the mad and hungry dogs, making their mock at our accursed lot.

If we must die, O let us nobly die,

So that our precious blood may not be shed in vain; then even the monsters we defy shall be constrained to honor us though dead! O Kinsmen! We must meet the common foe! Though outnumbered let us show us brave, and for their thousand blows deal one death blow!

What though before us lies the open grave? Like men we'll face the murderous, cowardly pack, pressed to the wall, dying, but fighting back!"

-If We Must Die, Claude McKay 1919

***

"We want freedom for all Black men held in federal, state, county and city prisons and jails."

"We believe that all black people should be released from the many jails and prisons because they have not received a fair and impartial trial."

Fatal force is not the only tactic employed by the power structure to our detriment. Another stratagem utilized is mass incarceration, since its very inception had the dual function of both bringing blacks back under the grips of forced labor and pursuing capitalistic agendas, this was made possible with the introduction of the 13th Amendment. As far back as the "Reconstruction Era" (1865-1876,) after the Civil War had ended and slaves became freemen the distraught, avaricious businessman and plantation owners alike sought out alternative avenues to produce a cheap labor force as close to the one previously lost, and incarceration seemed to be the consensus. In 1865, the "Black Codes" were created in the South (though Northerners had set forth laws of their own directed at blacks.) These outrageous, oppressive "laws" made the newly freed men susceptible to incarceration; in many respects akin to the slavery system they recently emerged from. Chicago, Illinois constructed a "law" that forbid blacks from out of town to visit there past a ten-day period, and if found out that such a grace period had expired and the out-of-towner still remained, he faced jail time and/or a stiff fine. Jails then contracted out its "prisoners" for labor purposes, so blacks brought into these jails, for violations of the Black Codes, were swiftly ushered into the hands of the avaricious businessman (or plantation owner) to supplement their need for workers. Likewise, if the black man was fined he was auctioned off to the highest bidder, likely a plantation owner (or greedy businessman) for whom he would toil until the price of his transgression was fulfilled. In some Southern states, these unfortunate brothers were addressed as servants and had to address their boss as master.

Even though the Black Codes and Jim Crow laws are technically no more, in present times the prison system has still seen significant expansion. Though the black man was first to bear the excruciating weight and bitter taste of prison, he is not currently the only one being captured (or held for ransom) and thrown behind bars. As today's statistics suggest, black youth and black women have increasingly become a part of the American prison system's appetite.

Like the slavery system, the prison system does not discriminate between man, woman, and child. However, to a great degree, many have stopped themselves short of fully comparing both systems. Maybe they see no need for comparison or maybe there is no comparison. If so, perhaps this can be attributed to the fact that prisons, unlike slavery, seem to be the only true "colorblind" institution within American society. Poor and uneducated whites in rural areas, along with Hispanics and Native Americans, have all seen their incarceration rates increase as the years have unfolded. On the other hand, maybe it's attributed to the lack of experience with imprisonment that hinders certain individuals from considering the aspects of both systems. Either way, one need only to consider the passage of the 13th Amendment (The Exception Clause) to realize the slavery system never truly met its death upon the signing of the Emancipation Proclamation:

"Neither slavery nor involuntary servitude except as a punishment for crime whereof the party shall have been duly convicted, shall exist within the United States or any place subject to their jurisdiction"

Forever the survivor, slavery has hidden itself within the "Exception Clause" of the 13th Amendment. Of course, our old foe no longer goes by his true name. This should come as no surprise as the brilliant Frederick Douglass fore-warned:

"Slavery has been fruitful in giving itself names. It has been called 'the peculiar institution', the social system, and the 'impediment'... it has been called by a great many names, and it will call itself by yet another name; and you and I and all of us had better wait and see what new form the Old Master will assume. In what new skin this Old Snake will come forth next."

When people are made slaves by law, prisoners will inherit the slave mentality. The slave mentality gives the slave, by rank and by definition a place inferior to that of their "keepers." No matter how smart he may be, the slave mentality will pressure him to become dependent rather than independent and such is also true for the prisoner. He will depend, some happily so, on his keepers to now feed him, clothe him, and tell him who he is (an inmate) and what's wrong and right. Similar to the slave, the prisoner's keeper strictly controls what the prisoner eats, what the prisoner wears, where the prisoner goes, who the prisoner sees, and the amount of rest the prisoner can get.

Sadly enough, once certain prisoners are befriended by their keepers the dark clouds in his life are painted the brightest blue, at least socially. Due to the undying gratitude the prisoner will have for his captors, when ill treatment is incurred he will make up an excuse however flimsy to justify the captor's motives and actions. Ironically, this very same individual will kneel down and pray to his God about his troubled heart, never once realizing that change will never happen as long as he's a willing participant in his own submission. In this manner, if not cautious, prisoners become emotionally infantilized over time.

It can also be stated that the relationship of power that existed in slave society between master and slave mirrors that of incarcerated society, between that of "inmates" and "administrators." In slave society the master, through force or the threat of force, wielded total power whilst the slaves remained totally powerless. This relationship of power allowed, among other things, the master to maintain production of goods as well as the upkeep of the plantation, without lifting a single finger. Those who refused to work for their master's benefit or were caught shirking their "duties" were brutalized to dissuade others from doing the same. Likewise, prisoners in incarcerated society find themselves within a similar relationship of domination for similar reasons. Inmates in whatever prison they find themselves, maintain that institution. The inmates cook, they clean, they sweep, they wash, they sow, they repair, and they even harvest. As it now stands, the inmate population removes the responsibility of all labor from the administration, as did slaves their masters.

Some may be naive to the fact that incarcerated individuals are under a constant threat of violence. Twenty-four hours of the day there circles the prison complex, not one but two "gun trucks" armed with M-16's and/or shotguns. However, though the threat of violence (even death) is ever present, violence is not the chief tactic employed by keepers to sustain the current arrangement. Non-participants are met with segregation (SHU-time) and/or have their stay in prison extended by way of having their "good time" credits withdrawn, which without question persuades others away from non-participation.

If a prisoner, overwhelmed mentally by his circumstances and condition, tries to escape such an existence his keepers turn "death squad" and strike him down with a "Hail of Bullets."

However, there would be no repercussions, no suspensions, no mourn for loss of life or public outcry.

This is because the prisoner, similar to the slave, has no socially-recognized existence outside of the institution which constrains him.

***

"We want education that teaches us our true history and our role in present-day society"

"We believe in an educational system that will give our people a knowledge of self. If a man does not have knowledge of himself and his position in society and the world, then he has little chance to relate to anything else."

--Black Panther's Ten Point Program (#5)

Throughout years of formal education, little is taught of heroes and heroines of black and brown people. There was no study or even mention of the highly intelligent Marcus Mossiah Garvey and the rapid international growth of the Universal Negro Improvement Association (U.N.I.A.) no acknowledgement of Sojourner Truth and her involvement with women's rights, while still championing freedom; neither was there mention of John Henrik Clarke, who vigorously taught the importance of knowing history:

"History is a clock that people use to tell their cultural and political time of day. It is a compass that people use to find themselves on the map of human geography. History is to people what a mother is to her child. Most importantly history tells a people where they are and where they still must go."

With history having such an enormous impact on the development and sustainment of a people, why is it that African history (our history) a major part of world history is so conveniently left out of the American educational system? Especially when considering how diverse American society is, we must demand and accept a full history of all our citizens. Anything less is willfully ignorant and erases an entire section of humanity.

Rudolphf R. Windsor, in his writing, "The Valley of Dry Bones" contends that it was intentionally done to create within us an inferiority complex:

"Some of us don't know our great history; because our oppressors deprived us of it; they distorted our history, deliberately and systematically misinterpreted our history and flavored it with race prejudice in order to leave us with an inferiority complex."

In "The Mis-Education of the Negro," by Carter G. Woodson, he puts forth a similar argument with a more descriptive view:

"the same educational process which inspires and stimulates the oppressor with the thought that he is everything and has accomplished everything worthwhile, depresses and crushes at the same time the spark of genius in the negro by making him feel that his race does not amount to much and never will measure up to the standards of other people… the inferiority of the negro is drilled into him in almost every class he enters and in almost every book he studies."

Of course, there are those who push back with the position that minorities are being taught exactly what everybody else in America are being taught. However, therein lies the problem, the difference between black and brown Americans and everybody else in America, is that other racial groups have a working knowledge of their true history, religion, and culture. Black and brown people in America, not being so 'equipped', find themselves void of support and re-enforcement in terms of personality and self-esteem. As a consequence, they have to falsely identify and find encouragement in a history, religion, and culture not of their own.

Unable to find their true personality and self-esteem they, over time, become functional inferiors. By becoming functional inferiors through the educational process it leaves them not only susceptible to external control, but also hinders their development as functional adults, functional spouses, and functional parents (the destruction of the family unit.) Additionally, black and brown Americans will display unbecoming characteristics, such as the practice of individualism; a feature that ultimately prevents the pursuit of group interests.

Black and brown people find themselves in a dissimilar situation than others. Naturally they must, for their own benefit, construct an education for themselves that deals effectively with their current state of condition. Wherefore, the history of their greatness (and failures) must be taught to them so they may find pride in their identity and culture (building self-esteem) live without parroting their mistakes and plow an economic path forward. So when:

"It is claimed that your race is doomed to economic inferiority, you may confidently look to the home of your ancestors and say that you have set out to recover for the colored people the strength that was their own before they set foot on the shores of this continent. You may say that you go to work with bright hopes, and that you will not be discouraged by the slowness of your progress; for you have to recover not only what has been lost in transplanting the negro race from its native soil to this continent, but you must reach higher levels than your ancestors ever had attained."

-Professor Franz Boas, "Commencement address at Atlanta University," May 31, 1906

***

Today, it seems, to be exposed to our beautiful history (though not void of setbacks) one must take a "special curriculum" or attend some specific college course. Undoubtedly, we fare much better with such studies in place. However, they do not go far enough. I'm of the persuasion that the beginning of progress lies in educational courses and/or studies of African history, culture, and folklore that begins at the preschool level, and carries over through grade school. This will offer us a defense against inferiorization. Sadly, our opponents are one step ahead of such a structural program at least within the existing educational system. In 2010, the conservatives in Arizona enacted HB 2281; a law that prohibits the teaching of "ethnic studies" (i.e., black history) in public schools, alleging that such an education teaches hate. This is not about hate teaching, special privileges, nor another group's shameful past, but instead about ending the continued victimization of a people. Remember "anything you don't control can be used as a weapon against you. Education is used as a weapon against you," (H. Rap Brown).

Whether it is a slavery system, Jim Crow laws, The Black Codes; shooting deaths of unarmed black and brown men, women, and children, mass incarceration and its psychological damages; or the mis-education of our youth, the unavoidable truth is, minorities have been catching all types of hell here in America.

Kaepernick's stance is just another form of defense; shining an all-consuming light on the brutality, ill-treatment, and frequent incidents of untimely deaths blacks (and other minorities) in America face on a constant basis; and though his platform has been undoubtedly stripped away, and consequently, his voice somewhat weakened, many have joined the chorus vocalizing his demands. As we now know for certain that:

"Power concedes nothing without demand. It never did and it never will. Find out just what any people will quietly submit to and you have found out the exact measure of injustice and wrong which will be imposed upon them, and these will continue till they are resisted with either words or blows, or with both. The limits of tyrants are prescribed by the endurance of those whom they oppress."

-Frederick Douglass

It is incumbent upon those morally grounded to never remain silent in the presence of oppression; to be forever vigilant and outspoken, highlighting such atrocities whenever they are uncovered in our society.

CHAPTER 10

The Perfect Platform

"If we think we have ours and don't owe any time or effort to help those left behind then we are a part of the problem rather than the solution to the fraying social fabric that threatens all Americans."

-Marian Wright Edelman

Music and Television

When T.I. appeared on national television and was asked why rappers glorify violence, but are quick to call out injustices T.I. in an extremely sincere and eloquent manner replied, "I think people need to take into consideration that hip hop traditionally has always been a reflection of the environment the artist had to endure before he made it to where he was. So, if you want to change the content of the music, change the environment of the artist and he won't have such negative things to say." These words ring true, for a young child whose vision is obscured by an impoverished, drug-and crime-ridden environment. The child is led to believe that the options available to them are limited to selling drugs, violence, and other criminal activities. Children learn from a number of various mediums; parents, peers, television, music, and their overall environment. As a race we are influenced by these factors, and when we observe hip hop artists, television characters, and the men in our neighborhoods these figures will inevitably become our role models. It then stands to reason that children will aspire to be the object of their affection. "I do not expect the white media to create positive black images," (Huey P. Newton.)

Hip hop has always played an integral role in influencing and educating people by replicating our ancestor's oral tradition of sharing information and stories. For example, KRS-One had a song called "The Sound of the Police" which explored the origins of police and how they morphed into existence from their inception of being enforcers during the times of slavery to their oppressive enforcement within impoverished neighborhoods, specifically, black impoverished neighborhoods. KRS-One highlighted the scary similarities between the past and present and the institutions that existed then and now. As a result of systemic racism perpetuated by a government, police, and society we have become a self-fulfilling prophecy. Rather than use music to uplift, educate, and empower our people we consistently support self-degradation with the glorification of the worst aspects of our existence, by perpetuating and idolizing violence, drug dealers, and the continual sexualization of our women.

It is therefore imperative that our conscious artists, entertainers, and people in media use their position to rally people and forge alliances to redress the imbalance within our society. We are no longer unfairly targeted solely based on the color of our skin, as Chuck D says in his book, *Fight the Power*: "It's very important for athletes and entertainers, especially black men, to say something uplifting and inspirational whenever they get an opportunity, because many children do not see strong black men in their community." We can't ever demand that others see us as anything more than the most derogatory examples of black people if our own vision of self is obscured. Kaepernick's #takeaknee is a prime example of an athlete having used their platform to highlight the issues that are prevalent to black people and demand that we are seen as more than the color of skin and are afforded equal rights. This is something that music has always fed into. By identifying what we want, need, and deserve as a people and taking our lead from activists like Kaepernick, Patrisse Cullors and others of that ilk we can effect change within ourselves and our music and change the narrative of the soundtrack to our world. For example, hip hop/rap has always reflected the political agenda in some fashion, and as incarceration has played a vital role in the lives of black people, in both the UK and USA, hip hop too has acknowledged the impact of imprisonment as dictated by the leader of that time.

There is little to no research, evidence or statistical proof that black people are more inclined to use or sell drugs than their white peers, yet they are more likely to be arrested and given a longer sentence for such crimes. Prison reform is now becoming more of a pressing issue for hip hop and it would seem as if Kaepernick's protest can be thanked for keeping this issue current and on the lips of influential people within media and entertainment. Such as Van Jones and his consistent activism and Jay Z who made a documentary about Kalief Browder and the necessity for bail reform.

Hip hop has always demonstrated political awareness and been closely linked to the issues of criminal justice, for example the song "Belly of the Beast," which was recorded by a prisoner whilst incarcerated and Public Enemy, infamous for their political music, performing on Rikers Island. However, with the explosion of social media and the internet enabling millions to be reached, people with a very real platform and involvement in entertainment are attracting more and more awareness to these issues. Meek Mill himself wrote a song entitled, "Young Black America," which explored the issue of the prison industry and its racially-biased sentences that inexplicably create a revolving door of repeat offenders, highlighting the criminalization of people's blackness. The tone of this song is now a reality for Meek Mill, who has been a victim of a racially-biased justice system. If we work together to minimize the inherent indoctrination that our children are raised with then we can begin to address the imbalance and decrease the incessant social and economic deprivation of their environment. The fundamental foundations of us as a people: our culture, values, and morals are non-existent. We no longer educate the younger generations with the knowledge that they have the strength to achieve, can dream big, and it is better to fail whilst trying than to never try at all. With real education our children can acquire knowledge, with knowledge they can learn, develop, and solidify the necessary skills required for life. With the absence of this knowledge, the wisdom to implement these tools into a more positive and progressive future is missing.

John Singleton highlighted the realities of our communities in his movie, "Boys N the Hood," when he successfully brought attention to the ongoing situation that black communities endure on a daily basis when the character Furious Styles gave his monologue. "...What we need to do is keep everything in our neighborhood, everything black. Black-owned with black money, just like the Jews, the Italians, the Mexicans, and the Koreans do... Well, how you think crack rock gets into the country? We don't own any planes. We don't own any ships. We are not the people who are flyin' and floatin' that shit in here. I know every time you turn on the TV that's what you see black people selling the rock, pushing the rock, pushing the rock, yeah, I know. But that wasn't a problem as long as it was here, wasn't a problem until it was in Iowa and it showed up on Wall Street where there are hardly any black people. Now if you want to talk about uh, guns, why is it that there is a gun shop on almost every corner in this community?... Tell you why, for the same reason that there's, a liquor store on almost every corner in the black community. Why? They want us to kill ourselves. You go out to Beverly Hills you don't see that shit. But they want us to kill ourselves. Yeah, the best way you can destroy a people, you take away their ability to reproduce themselves. Who is it that's dyin' out here on these streets every night? Y'all. Young brothers like yourselves. You doin' exactly what they want you to do. You have to think young brother, about your future, huh?"

Boyz N the Hood was made in 1991, but this monologue is as powerful and meaningful as at any time in our history. As a people, we are limited in our ability to reproduce due to drug abuse, alcoholism, violence, and incarceration. We lack the skills, ability, and often the knowledge of how to break the cycle but more importantly than that we lack the willingness to demonstrate black pride and come together to build strong communities once more. Very often we fail to support black-owned businesses with black money in spite of black people's spending power having increased considerably since 2000; and it is estimated that $1.3 trillion is spent solely by the black community, with the vast majority of this money going anywhere except to specifically black-owned businesses.

***

First Amendment Fighter: Luther "Uncle Luke" Campbell

Pioneer: One who goes before, preparing the way for others, as an early settler.

Art imitates life and life imitates art. Music has always been a way for artists to artistically portray their realities. Whether it was Lil Kim and Biggie with their graphic lyrics or N.W.A. with their "Fuck the Police" record, hip hop has always been the genre that has caused controversy in households, radio stations or record stores. Free speech under the First Amendment made that possible.

There is always someone who prepares the way for others. These people are referred to as pioneers and that's exactly who Uncle Luke was for "southern" rap and hip hop, especially when rap began transcending barriers and entering the homes of the white demographic at alarming rates. For white America, outside influences don't pertain to them unless it affects their agendas, status quo or influences their youth. As rap started crossing over into other areas outside of the African-American and Latino communities, it became a serious problem for the rest of society.

Luther Roderick Campbell (born 1960) a.k.a "Luke Skywalker" is an African-American record label owner, rap performer, promoter, and actor. Most known for being the leader of the rap group "2 Live Crew" The sexual content of the lyrics his group produced caused controversy and eventually lead to a legal battle. Uncle Luke was not an original member of the group, but through Luke they became known as southern rappers. It was after their shot as a California rap crew, Luke brought them down for a show that piqued his interest which eventually led to Luke becoming their hype-man/manager.

Uncle Luke was an entrepreneur and owned his own label "Luke Skywalker Records," which was eventually changed to "Luke Records" as George Lucas filed a law suit for infringing on the name of his Star Wars character, Luke Skywalker. Uncle Luke was a concert promoter who brought popular rappers to the city of Miami in the early 80's. Luke also took an eight-week study course at a public radio station, WNDA, learning basic audio editing and production techniques, which would go on to assist him in his music career.

Uncle Luke's first solo LP, "Banned in the USA," was a 2 Live Crew record, released under the new Luke handwritten "Tan" label, which was sold out of his car. The lyrical content of the 2 Live Crew album was challenged in the courts. It was a parody case, Uncle Luke would lose in the district court and he would lose an obscenity trial in federal court. The courts deemed their music obscene. Uncle Luke would eventually take the lower courts all the way to the Supreme Court seeking freedom of speech, eventually having his case overturned. Without Uncle Luke going to the extent that he did and putting up a fight within the court system, case precedent would have been established to silence us. Some of our favorite songs, such as Future's "Mask Off" or Nikki Minaj's "Anaconda" would have been deemed obscene and pulled off the shelves and internet at their discretion.

Parody: a humorous imitation of literary or music.

The First Amendment, which protects parody, ultimately makes it difficult for the courts to object. These are reasons comedians on Saturday Night Live (SNL) can make jokes imitating others. Uncle Luke should be thanked, because the pressure he had to face at a young age could have been overwhelming. Being his own record executive and owning his own record company, Uncle Luke started selling records in white communities, white households, to white children, and performing at predominantly white concerts. It's easy to see why he received so much pushback. He was a young black man challenging the status quo, as hip hop was not viewed as acceptable nor was it respected at that time.

Uncle Luke explained why he fought: "My whole thing was, and the reason that I made the fight is basically I said, hey listen, here's a good situation. I'm seeing 20 years from now. I'm seeing that white kids like hip hop, then white kids get a good understanding of how black kids are living and then there wouldn't be any separation. It'll actually bring races together much more than anything. So, when I walk on South Beach I hear these kids playing music, everybody wearing the same clothes, I know it's a whole different appreciation. When I look at everything that's what I fought for, everybody to be the same."

I think it's imperative we honor our legends while they are alive and well and able to enjoy the appreciation, such as BET awarding Uncle Luke with the Honorary Award: Uncle Luke saved hip hop and did what so many others are reluctant to do. He invested his money wisely and put his time and energy into building up the community and the youth.

Uncle Luke said: "In 35 years in this business ain't nobody ever honored me for shit." As Uncle Luke gathered his thoughts and held back tears he continued: "I took my first check 35 years ago and bought my mama a house. My second check, I started my youth program for kids like Devonte Freeman, who can play in the program and then go play in the fucking Super Bowl. That's real shit." Luke said, referring to his Liberty City Optimist organization: "You would think they would call and say, 'Hey Luke you're doing some philanthropical shit.' They ain't call, because they wanted me to be small. I'ma say shit right at the end of the day: I started hip hop in the South." (Luke's wife brokered the deal for Devonte Freeman to become the highest paid running back in the NFL.)

The respect and admiration for Uncle Luke has skyrocketed for me. Some may never get a chance to experience or know what it's like living in the ghetto. Uncle Luke gives us a way out through his football league, which teaches us more than just football; we are taught life lessons that we will take with us into manhood. That's why you see Devonte Freeman continuing that mentorship by coming home to hold free functions and football camps for the next generation.

Uncle Luke is cut from a different type of cloth, and it seems they don't make that type of fabric anymore. Uncle Luke challenged white America, hip hop and the U.S. Supreme Court by getting his obscenity ruling overturned. In the midst of resistance, glory often comes when the smoke clears, sometimes too late. I thank Uncle Luke for his contributions and we love and honor him. It's these instances of resistance that propels brothers like Kaepernick forward, because they are assured that in the end they are not alone.

"What this does is let black folk know the First Amendment really does apply to us. It says we can speak our mind the same way white people do."

-Uncle Luke

EXCERPTS: 'I WILL NOT BE COMPLICIT'

Excerpts from Sen. Jeff Flake's remarks Tuesday from the floor of the U.S. Senate, as prepared for delivery.

"Mr. President, I rise today to address a matter that has been much on my mind, at a moment when it seems that our democracy is more defined by our discord and our dysfunction than it is by our values and our principles. Let me begin by noting a somewhat obvious point that these offices that we hold are not ours to hold indefinitely. We are not here simply to mark time. Sustained incumbency is certainly not the point of seeking office. And there are times when we must risk our careers in favor of our principles."

"We must never regard as "normal" the regular and casual undermining of our democratic norms and ideals. We must never meekly accept the daily sundering of our country — the personal attacks, the threats against principles, freedoms, and institutions; the flagrant disregard for truth or decency, the reckless provocations, most often for the pettiest and most personal reasons, reasons having nothing whatsoever to do with the fortunes of the people that we have all been elected to serve."

"Reckless, outrageous, and undignified behavior has become excused and countenanced as 'telling it like it is,' when it is actually just reckless, outrageous, and undignified. And when such behavior emanates from the top of our government, it is something else: It is dangerous to a democracy. Such behavior does not project strength — because our strength comes from our values. It instead projects a corruption of the spirit, and weakness."

"Mr. President, I rise today to say: Enough. We must dedicate ourselves to making sure that the anomalous never becomes normal. With respect and humility, I must say that we have fooled ourselves for long enough that a pivot to governing is right around the corner, a return to civility and stability right behind it. We know better than that."

"When we remain silent and fail to act when we know that that silence and inaction is the wrong thing to do — because of political considerations, because we might make enemies, because we might alienate the base, because we might provoke a primary challenge, because ad infinitum, ad nauseum — when we succumb to those considerations in spite of what should be greater considerations and imperatives in defense of the institutions of our liberty, then we dishonor our principles and forsake our obligations. Those things are far more important than politics."

"The notion that one should stay silent as the norms and values that keep America strong are undermined and as the alliances and agreements that ensure the stability of the entire world are routinely threatened by the level of thought that goes into 140 characters — the notion that one should say and do nothing in the face of such mercurial behavior is ahistoric and, I believe, profoundly misguided."

"The principles that underlie our politics, the values of our founding, are too vital to our identity and to our survival to allow them to be compromised by the requirements of politics. Because politics can make us silent when we should speak, and silence can equal complicity. I have children and grandchildren to answer to, and so, Mr. President, I will not be complicit."

B.Smith, A. Rivera, M. Mombranche, L. Stephens

CHAPTER 11

Mr. Unpatriotic

"The Nazi symbol is what militaries fought against in World War II so to say that White Supremacists can be nice people and not call them a Hate Group is unpatriotic because the Second World War was about fighting oppression and hate."
-Beverley Smith

One of the very first people that found himself on the receiving end of a most vicious attack by then-candidate Trump, in front of a national audience, was our United States Senator, military veteran, and American hero John McCain (R.I.P) In Trump's estimate, John McCain was found to be lacking and less than the courageous hero we all know him to be for the simple fact that the now-U S Senator was a prisoner of war or as Trump so rudely put it: because he got caught. This was an extremely unpatriotic statement. Indeed, to condemn an American war hero on the basis of his capture by the enemy (the nation's enemies) while fighting for the liberties we all enjoy is unmistakably unpatriotic, un-American, and stains America's moral leadership position in the world.

Many Americans did not share Trump's assessment of John McCain, but they still supported him and his words as mere "campaign strategy." However, we cannot continue justifying the actions of a man that continuously proves himself unworthy of our respect simply based on the fact that he is now the president, as such would undoubtedly compromise the principles of any self-respecting American. We should not be willing to endure internal, moral conflict nor suffer in silence as the president stands before the world and makes a mockery of the office he holds in representing this great nation. As Americans, we have an inherent duty and moral obligation to reject and oppose any hint of moral bankruptcy in our country's highest office.

Of course, there are those who would contend that we all should accord president Trump a level of respect based solely on the fact that he occupies the highest office in America. Those who are of this persuasion display in themselves a failure to understand, as H. Rap. Brown once pointed out, "Individuals, not positions, merit respect."

Coincidently, those very same "Trump supporters" seem to feel the most disrespected and discontent, not with the unpatriotic ways of president Trump, but instead with Kaepernick's and other· prominent NFL players kneeling while the national anthem plays. These seemingly confused individuals also maintain that they support the freedoms afforded by the United States to its citizens, including the right to peacefully protest against racial inequality, racial injustice, and the general mistreatment of black and brown Americans.

Disagreeable to their taste it seems, is just the manner in which it is done. It is the discontented position that protesting the national anthem is not the "right" way to effectuate the desired results we so passionately seek. We must not be persuaded in the slightest by such outside opinions; not only because we are not bound by the opinions of others, but also as George Jackson has advised that in struggle: "no tactic can be ignored or discounted." Furthermore, how can they "profess to favor freedom," said Frederick Douglass, and "deprecate agitation?" These individuals, Mr. Douglass goes on to say, "Are men who want crops without plowing up the ground." If one truly prefers freedom for all Americans, regardless of color or racial background, then they must prefer to have it even in the mist of traditional attitudes.

Attention should be paid to the subtle suggestions placed before us to choose our leaders. In mid-October 2017, certain sports anchors such as Herm Edwards, Will Cain, and the sort were very adamant about supplanting Kaepernick with Malcom Jenkins and/or Michael Bennet. While I do not take issue with the capabilities of either of these fine brothers to engage in earnest struggle in effectuating the immediate and long-term change necessary, the question must be asked: why the sudden push for change in leadership? Some would argue that Kaepernick's persona is too reminiscent of black America's militant history. That his display of the proud afro and the unrelenting Black Power fist or the infamous socks speaking in unmistakable terms of their disdain for "pigs" (rogue police) all are symbols suggesting the re-emergence of a long thought forcibly repressed decades ago.

Others argue that the NFL owners are so control-obsessed that they cannot deal with the reality or a public perception that they were not, at all times, in absolute control of the protests. That their perception of control would be shattered and remain in pieces if Kaepernick were inclusive at the "round table" and therefore, instrumental in the outcome of the terms ultimately agreed upon between the Players Coalition and the NFL. He would appear as a shining figure, supported by the many that changed "business as usual" within the all-powerful NFL. That narrative does not allow the "concerned majority," nor the media to praise the NFL while they arrogantly pat themselves on the back for initiating progress. For them, nothing outside of hand-picking protest leaders delivering the terms that must be agreed upon, and "black-balling" agitators will suffice; as they cannot, in the words of Bob McNair, "let the prisoners run the asylum."

I believe that it is not an issue of being for or against one argument or the other, but that truth can be found somewhere in between both viewpoints. The strategic image and militant mentality put forth by Kaepernick, to some, may be very disconcerting and troubling. This coupled with the NFL's fear of losing control of the issue has caused such a discomfort as to warrant, among those involved, a strong counter-strategy; one that replaces Kaepernick, the protest's authentic mouthpiece, with NFL players who would seem not to embody such a resistant spirit to some kind of owner-favorable compromise. This belief is bolstered by the statement made by Malcom Jenkins that he will no longer kneel for the anthem due to the NFL's generous financial contributions; to which another Players Coalition member, Eric Reid, stated: "He does not speak for them." Without questioning any Players Coalition member's loyalty to the ultimate objective, the NFL and sport shows constant support of some players over Kaepernick must be given attention by all involved in the solution, and other interested parties, as a "divide and conquer" techniques as these tactics have plagued our righteous movements for centuries. Therefore, we must remain forever mindful of not only this useful tool wielded to destroy our aims but also our ultimate objective moving forward.

However, regardless of the outcome of the "Players' Protest," Kaepernick has already paid the most severe penalty for his love of the people; which is his ability to play and earn a handsome living, doing the one other thing we are all certain he loves and enjoys: football. However, in using his platform to inspire social justice, while risking "career suicide," brother Kaepernick has enjoined himself amongst great company.

Paul Robeson (1898-1976) born in Princeton, New Jersey by the age of seventeen earned himself a scholarship to attend Rutgers University making just the third African-American to do so. His talent for sports, like Kaepernick, emerged on the football field gaining him a spot on the All-American football team. Despite his football prowess and the recognition that sprang from such a talent, Mr. Robeson remained a race-conscious man. This was evident early on from a statement made by him in respect to, it seems, his determination to persevere and represent.

"When I was out on the football field or in a classroom or just anywhere else, I was not there just on my own. I was representative of a lot of Negro boys who wanted to play football and wanted to go to college, and as their representative, I had to show that I could take whatever was handed out."

Unfortunately, what was "handed out" was racism, as on his first day as a freshman player on Rutger's football team, his white teammates tried to kill him. This would not be Mr. Robeson's last run-in with racism. After graduating Columbia University law school (using his pro-football earnings to pay his tuition) in 1923 Mr. Robeson took up the practice of law within a firm. His professional career as a skilled lawyer was short-lived as, yet again, racism plagued his work environment.

In 1924, with the support of his wife/manager, Mr. Robeson turned to performance. This proved to be the right move, as he quickly ascended to fame. First by becoming wildly popular for his performance as Shakespeare's Othello, followed up by his big screen appearance in African American director Oscar Micheaux's "Body and Soul" in 1925. Despite his fame and comfortable living situation, Mr. Robeson could not ignore the condition plaguing the rest of his people, including not only those living within America, but also those who lived in other nations. He started using his platform and fame to address "black struggle" in all parts of the world, its interconnectedness and our collective responsibility to end it. Such is recognizable in his writing "Africa Call-Will you help?" where he suggests that Africans in America give concrete support and align themselves with the black struggle in Africa on which, he asserts, our "full freedom" depends:

"But Negros who have not lost all pride and dignity know that if we are at all serious about our full freedom here in America we must understand what the future of Africa means... their freedom and dignity will be of immeasurable assistance in our final break-through here in these United States..."

In Mr. Robeson's political opinion, the complete support of Africa by Africans living in America is a prerequisite for a free, independent, and powerful African continent and that such a development would prove extremely beneficial to Africans living in other nations, namely in the U.S.

"A new Africa will mean in the end a new Alabama, a new Mississippi, Arkansas, Georgia, a new Washington D.C. for us"

Here it seems Mr. Robeson was envisioning all Africans, particularly within the U.S., coming up under not only the protection of a centralized, globally recognized African government but also directly connected and supported by its abundance of resources, finally finding themselves accorded the human dignity and respect common to all other races. This, to a certain extent, Mr. Robeson felt he had already found in Russia as opposed to the United States. The appreciation felt by Mr. Robeson led him to take a particular interest in Russia, visiting there several times, studying their language as well as folk culture and ultimately developing political ties. Forever his outspoken self and capable of picking his own "friends," at a 1949 Paris peace gathering conference, he spoke in earnest interest of black people as their representative, stating that:

"It was unthinkable that American Negros would go to war on behalf of those who have oppressed us for generations... against a country which in one generation has raised our people to full human dignity of mankind."

Such a statement didn't go over well with the "American Majority" and was taken as a betrayal to America, especially within the existing Cold War climate. He was vilified, criticized, and regarded as un-American. Even the great Jackie Robinson spoke out against his statement saying, to the un-American activities committee, that Robeson did not speak for the American Negro and that the Negro not fighting for America "sounded silly." In his autobiography, Jackie Robinson admits that his words to the committee were regrettable:

"In those days I had much more faith in the ultimate justice of the American white man then I have today. I would reject such an invitation if offered now. I have grown wiser and closer to the painful truths about America's destructiveness and I do have increased respect for Paul Robeson who, over a span of twenty years, sacrificed himself, his career and the wealth and comfort he once enjoyed because, I believe, he was sincerely trying to help his people."

Like Mr. Robinson, Kaepernick has sacrificed his career and the comfort he once enjoyed because he too is sincerely trying to help his people. What's striking about both these great men is that their stance wasn't deferred in the slightest by the thought of their earning potential being lost or at the very least hindered. In America we have become all too comfortable with the genuine sacrifice of others being belittled and regarded as unwise. While not fully understanding that change, whether personal or to inspire others, both require earnest sacrifice. In biblical times a sacrifice was required to gain God's favor, and the fact is, Kaepernick has given the greatest of all sacrifices: himself. As time inches forward and the progress and awareness his stance created comes into full view, history will undoubtedly reveal he was favored by the highest.

CHAPTER 12

Trump-ism

Ism-n. a distinctive doctrine, cause or theory. b. a manner of action or behavior characteristic of a specific person or thing (animalism). c. prejudice or discrimination on the basis of a (specified) attribute (racism) (sexism). 2. a. abnormal state, or condition resulting; from excess of a (specified) thing (alcoholism). 3 a. a doctrine or theory: cult peculiar feature or trait (colloquialism).

"It's called an American Dream because you have to be asleep to believe it!" -George Carlin

First, I would like to explain to you what an -ism is. An -ism, as defined above will perfectly describe the characteristics of Donald J. trump; thus, "Trumpism." Trump is a truthful guy, not in the sense that he doesn't lie, but he can't help but be blunt with his questions, answers, and statements. The person he presents is who he is. Maya Angelou once said "If someone shows you who they are, believe them the first time." Trump talks straight words and he means what he says. He doesn't mind being brash and disrespectful. This is the way he sees things and he's perfected this behavior which he has turned into a craft through many years of doing business. He understands how to push buttons, what to say, and when to say it. It's the doctrine Trump has perfected. Trump-ism is bigger than Trump. It's an -ism.

October 7, 2016 during the presidential election, The Washington Post released a video and accompanying article about now-president Donald J. Trump and television host Billy Bush having "an extremely lewd conversation about women," in 2005. Now as you read this, understand that this is the man that United States citizens have elected as president, with all the facts present. In the video, Trump indicated that he might start kissing a woman that he and Bush were about to meet during the filming of an episode of "Access Hollywood" a show owned by NBC Universal.

The media dubbed this scandal "pussygate." Commentators and lawyers described such an action as sexual harassment. Trump tells Bush about a failed attempt to seduce Nancy O'Dell, who was Bush's co-host at the time:

"I moved on her and I failed I admit."

"I did try and fuck her. She was married."

"And I moved on her heavily, in fact I took her out furniture shopping. She wanted to get some furniture. I said "I'll show you where they have some nice furniture." I took her out I moved on her like a bitch. But I couldn't get there, and she was married. Then all of a sudden I see her, she's now got the big phony tits and everything. She totally changed her look." Later, referring to Adrianne Zucker (whom they were waiting to meet up with) Trump says: "I better use some tic-tac's just in case I start kissing her. You know I'm automatically attracted to beautiful women I just start kissing them. It's like a magnet. Just kiss. I don't even wait. And when you're a star, they let you do it. You can do anything. Grab 'em by the pussy. You can do anything."

For Trump, this is repetitive behavior. Twenty of Trump's former "Apprentice" employees described Trump's behavior towards women as lewd and inappropriate. Legal professionals have come out and interpreted the language of sexual assault as "touching a person's genitals without consent" (also known as groping) and is considered sexual assault in most jurisdictions in the U.S.

Lisa Bloom, a sexual harassment and civil rights lawyer, stated: "Let's be very clear, he is talking about sexual assault, he is talking about grabbing a woman's genitals without her consent."

Trump and some of his supporters denied the groping as sexual assault. During the campaign he has apologized for the video's content by deflecting saying, "Bill Clinton has said far worse on the golf course." These remarks provoked strong reactions. Majority leader Mitch McConnell, Trump's VP, and Republican National Committee Chairman Lance Preibus indicated their disapproval of Trump's words but did not renounce their support or call for his resignation. This is Trump-ism at its finest. Trump shrugged off the scandal as "locker room talk."

Those remarks prompted a separate dialogue in locker rooms across the nation. As an athlete, never have I heard someone boasting about sexual assault in the locker room. Republican Sen. John McCain stated that he would no longer support the ticket. House Speaker, Paul Ryan, announced that he would no longer defend or support Trump's campaign but Ryan never cashed in on his promises, failing to officially withdraw his endorsement for Trump. It's as if among the elites, the bottom line is all that matters (politics.) Bush resigned and faced major backlash for his engagement with Trump on the video. Trump, amid allegations and lawsuits, was handed the republican nomination and eventually elected as the 45th President of the United States of America.

Many others use their power and influence to do as they please. Trump isn't alone. Harry Weinstein and Bill O'Riley were just a few of the higher-profile people who abused their power and influence. O'Riley, one of the highest paid TV personalities, resigned from Fox amid sexual assault allegations. There were never any criminal charges filed, but plenty of settlements for undisclosed amounts. Settlements allude to guilt in my book. Fox was privy to O'Riley's allegations and settlements. At the time, Fox ratings must've been more important than women's voices, rights, and respect. It wasn't until their brand began to be smeared did they cut their losses with one of their highest rated shows. History shows us big businesses will overlook things and even silence accusers in order to protect their investments, but the truth always prevails.

Harvey Weinstein, a Hollywood elite with "power and status," has multiple accusers; so many that their photos (gathered together) would seem like a mural. On multiple occasions, Weinstein made advance after advance on multiple women inside and outside the industry. Women will not be disrespected and are fighting back. Taylor Swift and Lupita Nyongo caused Hollywood to re-examine itself and the way these allegations and situations are handled.

I recall a Trump supporter on Fox news saying: "Hillary spent a month talking about Trump's pussygate scandal but took over a week to speak out against Weinstein's actions, especially being that he was a big contributor of hers." Hillary should've come out immediately but when you have a commander-in-chief, leader of the free world who normalized his action despite his behavior and was supported all the way to the White House, it's just difficult to grasp. Chris Cumo said it best: "When you ignore it, you empower it." Everyone should be held to the same standards, some to even higher standards. Harry Weinstein stepped away from his company and business holdings, so should Trump. That's politics: polite-tricks.

Hijacker

Trump chose to insert himself into a battle that has nothing to do with him, and most people feel he hijacked the issue and made it about him and his rhetoric. In the first 100 days of his presidency, Trump was adamant about passing bills. His promises began to seem more difficult than just yelling at rallies, "We're going to build a wall" or "repeal and replace." The Senate and the House could not come up with enough votes to pass bills, so in order to deflect attention away from the mayhem between democrats and republicans, he inserted himself into the NFL & the players' protest. Let me put things in context for you because the media can blur the lines and leave out information to tailor the desired images they want to portray. There's been much talk of the players' protest during the national anthem being viewed as disrespect. The fashion in which the players chose to protest (kneeling) was highly criticized, but the reason behind the protest (inequality and injustice for black and brown people) seemed to never arise.

Star Spangled Banner...

"And where is the band so dauntingly swore, that the havoc of war and battles confusion. A home and country should never leave us no more? Their blood has washed out their footsteps with pollution. No refuge save the hireling and slave from terror of flight or the gloom of the grave. No, the Star-Spangled Banner in triumph doth wave. O er land of the free and home of the brave."

As an African American living in the United States, the Star-Spangled Banner is highly disrespectful and outrageously offensive. A song written by a slave owner, Francis Scott Key: "No refuge could save the hireling and slave." As descendants of slaves, that cuts to the core, knowing the hatred with which the Star-Spangled Banner was written. For me, putting my hand over my heart is disrespected to those who fought so diligently for the freedom of black and brown people in America. Why should I stand? The song is an insult to people of color because when I hear land of the free and home of the brave, I hear land of the thief and home of the slave. Equality will always be unattainable whilst one group continues to have the power to deny rights to others.

If you can justify paid patriotism, I would hope you can find justification on why Kaepernick took a knee. The Department of Defense paid the NFL to promote this fake sense of cultural hegemony and spread this false notion that we are on the same page. While those anthems may make Americans look like they are on the same page, behind the scenes there's a bigger story. Black and brown people are treated unequal, discriminated against, and are brutalized by police officers and the criminal justice system. Kaepernick took a knee during the national anthem not because he wanted to disparage the flag, but instead to bring scrutiny to the many ways in which black and brown people were being destroyed by police brutality. The names of the many victims that rang loud at Black Lives Matter rallies, on television news stations and in newspapers across America compelled Kaepernick to kneel.

In the past, black men who fought in WWI came home only to be beaten and lynched simply for refusing to surrender the sidewalk to white people. We must ask ourselves what flag did they serve under and why should we celebrate it? Especially when under this banner there is no justice nor equality for black and brown people in America. The enigma of loyalty is that blacks love a country that does not love them. We pledge allegiance to a flag that is drenched in black blood.

Kaepernick is supported because he echoed the many sentiments we all felt, but have yet to act on. A time will come where we will no longer be silent nor embody a flag that supports unjustified killing of our people at the hands of rogue police officers. We can fly this American flag and sing a tune of Kumbaya, but the reality remains that the American flag is drenched in black blood. I believe this is the reason we as a nation stay away from those pages of our history.

In a heightened healthcare battle, president Trump lacked the votes in congress to repeal or replace Obama Care. John McCain, on a deciding vote, chose not to support the bill that he felt would not benefit the American people. Trump knew things were looking bad for him on The Hill and quickly approaching his first year in office, he decided to divert attention. Trump, while speaking at a rally in Alabama on behalf of U.S Senator Luther Strange, said "Wouldn't you love to see these NFL owners, when someone disrespects our flag to say, 'Get that son of a bitch off the field right now. Out. He's fired.' You know, some owner is going to do that. He's going to say, 'That guy disrespects our flag, he's fired.' And that owner, they don't know it. They'll be the most popular person for a week. They'll be the most popular in the country."

The NFL reacted to the president's attack on the league. Almost 200 or more players subsequently took a knee, held a fist, sat or locked arms in solidarity. Although this sparked a new protest, it showed that owners and players wouldn't compromise on issues that have value to them. The entire Pittsburg Steelers team stayed in the locker room (except Army Vet Alejandra Villanueva.) The Seattle Seahawks did the same and issued a statement: "As a team, we decide we will not participate in the national anthem. We will not stand for the injustice that plagued people of color in this country. Out of the love of our country and in honor of the sacrifices made on our behalf, we unite to oppose those that would deny our most basic freedoms. We remain committed to walk towards equality and justice for all."

Even some of Trump's friends in the league pushed back against him.

Robert Kraft:

"I am deeply disappointed by the tone of the comments made by the president Friday. I am proud to be associated with so many players who make tremendous contributions of positivity impacting our communities. Their efforts, both on and off the field, help bring people together and make our community stronger. There is no greater unifier in this country than sports and unfortunately, nothing more divisive than politics. I think our political leaders could learn a lot from the lessons of team work and the importance of working together towards one common goal. Our players are intelligent, thoughtful and care deeply about our community and I support their right to peacefully effect social change and raise awareness in a manner that they feel is most impactful."

Tom Brady: "Yeah, I certainly disagree with what (Trump) said. I thought it was divisive."

Doug Baldwin: "I'm not surprised by Trump's comments he has shown from the beginning his dehumanizing nature. To think he would be any different is not to know reality of the presidency. He has surrounded himself with likeminded people and has removed anyone who challenges him. He acts like a child craving for attention and any attention will do."

@KingJames
"It's not about dividing. We as American people need to come together even stronger."

@MalcomJenkins
"This is not about the flag at all, this is as a concerned citizen. Trump doesn't know much about the guys who are behind those helmets."

@martysarusrex
"The idea of @DonaldTrump thinking that suggesting firing me from football, confirms he thinks that it's all I can do as a black man."

After Trump's divisive remarks "Get that son of a bitch of the field now." NASCAR (a predominately white sport) came out in support of Trump and his divisive remarks. NASCAR expressed that they would not tolerate any disrespecting of the flag, and those who don't stand would be reprimanded.

@RealDonaldTrump
"So proud of nascar and its supporters and fans. They won't put up with disrespecting our country or flag. They said it loud and clear."

Trump also sent vice president, Mike Pence, to a Colts game. Out of all Sundays, he chose a Sunday when all teams vowed to show unity and push back against Trump's "Get that son of a bitch of the field now" statement.

@VP
"Looking forward to cheering for our @colts and honoring the great career of #18 Peyton Manning."

I take issue with the vice president's action because he chose to use his position of power as a political ploy. All high-ranking government officials have their own secret service detail and their itineraries are usually pre-scheduled and situated for proper security measures. VP Mike Pence attended the Colt's game knowing that their opponents (San Francisco 49ers) initially sparked the protest and that they had players who had been kneeling all season. Pence announced beforehand if there was any disrespect he would leave. Pence had no intentions of watching the ceremony or the game. His pre-scheduled attendance was a publicity stunt and a photo op. Despite the vice president's attendance, both teams #tookaknee.

@VP

"I left today's Colts game because @Potus and I will not dignify any event that disrespects our soldiers, our flag or our National Anthem."

This attendance by the vice president was exactly what it was intended to be: a scheduled spectacle. Security was briefed in place for any imminent threat, the hallways were cleared and searched for any possible danger. The vice president may have fooled some, but he wasted tax payer's dollars to attend a game in which he knew the players would kneel. Recently, Pence cheered the NFL's decision to ban kneeling during the anthem by tweeting #Winning. Those sentiments were challenged by Kaepernick retweeting a legal citation posted by his attorney, Mark Gregas, which cites a section of the federal code from the Legal Information Institute prohibiting federal elected officials, including the president and vice president, from attempting to influence the hiring decisions of private employers on partisan grounds. The code states that any "covered government official" may face fines and up to 15 years in prison for acting to "influence, solely on the basis of partisan political affiliation, an employment decision or employment practice of any private entity."

I guess this administration is under the impression that they are above the law. This was definitely an attempt by the president and vice president to influence the NFL to mandate the players to stand, and not even a year later that's just what happened. Facts given, you decide their punishment for breaking the law: fine or prison, either or both will do for me.

ESPN's Jemelle Hill received a verbal reprimand for tweeting "Trump is a white supremacist" by her employers at ESPN, citing a company policy. Jemelle Hill also responded to Jerry Jones's statement that none of his players would kneel.

@JemelleHill

"This play always works: Change happens when advertisers are impacted. If you feel strongly about JJ's comments boycott his advertisers."

Prior to Jemelle Hill's tweet about Trump, the president tweeted that Hill should be fired for her comments. After Ms. Hill's second infraction, ESPN suspended her for her second violation to their social media guidelines. Rules are rules and if they are put in place and you knowingly break them, then I understand ESPN's swift action, but I do not agree with their rule. Especially, when you hire a man like Keith Olberman who also tweeted the president "fuck you @RealDonaldTrump Nazi Nazi fuck Nazi Nazi Racist Nazi bigot go fuck yourself fucking Nazi fuckers." I have a problem with this double standard. Everybody has someone they answer to. ESPN is regulated by the FCC, who in turn is regulated by the government, which ultimately leads back to Trump.

Hill spoke in our best interest and offered advice because she is as outspoken as she is intelligent when it comes to these issues and knows how to achieve desired results. It's very important for black people to speak on these issues for the black community, as more often than have other races tackle these issues which they have never dealt with personally.

When Hill's employer (ESPN) tried to silence her voice because she had a powerful platform, we in the black community should've come to her aid and flexed our power as consumers. We should've canceled subscriptions and harnessed our power and offered Hill her own show, a show where she would not be censored for speaking the truth. This is the first lesson, but that's not to say our white family can't speak on our behalf like Max Kellerman, Greg Popovich, Steve Kerr, Pastor Flagler, and others who are consistent in their views and remain "woke."

Ahead of the NFL Monday night football kickoff, legendary coach Mike Ditka weighed in on the national anthem protest. Speaking with NBC's Jim Gray, Ditka explained why he thinks millionaire football stars of all races and creeds have no reason to protest the flag. Ditka explained, "There has been no oppression in the last 100 years that I know of, now maybe I'm not following it as careful as other people. I think the opportunity is here for every race, religion, creed, color, and nationality. If you want to work, if you try, if you put the effort you can accomplish anything." It doesn't surprise me, but for a man who lived through the civil rights era to say "there's been no oppression in the last 100 years," that's a sign of a man who lives in a bubble. Besides modern-day oppression, I recall during the civil rights era people of color were sprayed with hoses, bitten by dogs, and beaten by police officers. Now it's as if those acts of hatred, discrimination, and racism have come full circle to the killing of unarmed black men and women, excessive force by police officers, and open acts of racism. There has not been one year in the last 100 years where people of color have not been oppressed. So where has Ditka been?

@RealDonaldTrump

"Many people booed the players who kneeled yesterday. These are the fans that demand respect for our flag."

Trump used the small percentage of people that booed to further his agenda by distracting the American people.

At a time when no legislation was passed and bills failed to even reach the Senate, Trump needed to divert attention. The real problem behind the scenes was that police shot and killed 492 people in the first part of the year (a number identical to the count for the same period of the prior two years, as of June 1, 2017.) The overall pace for 2017 was on track to approach 1,000 for the third year in a row.

Data shows police continue to kill a disproportionately large number of black males who account for a quarter of deaths, yet only 6% of the nation's population. Marian Edelman once said: "If we think we have ours and don't owe any time or money or effort to help those left behind, then we are a part of the problem rather than the solution to the fraying social fabric that threatens all Americans." That is why Kaepernick so graciously took a knee, he could no longer stand and watch from a place of privilege; he felt the urge that something had to be done.

John Edwards, a 15-year-old, was one of seven unarmed black males killed in Texas. He was shot in April of 2017 by a police officer in a Dallas suburb. An officer opened fire with an AR-15 rifle on Edwards and his friends as they drove away from a party, according to reports. The police department initially said the teens tried to back over the officer, but retracted their statements after officials viewed the video of the shooting. I wonder how many people must die before we realize as a society that we have a real problem with our perception, police training, and our policies.

Another grave danger in African American communities is· mental health. We lack the proper funding to assist officers with training tactics to de-escalate these encounters. Mental health continues to be a big factor in fatal shootings. A quarter of those killed had mental health issues of some sort. Seattle police shot and killed Charlene Lyles, a 30-year-old pregnant woman suffering from mental health issues, after she called 911 to report an attempted burglary at her home. Police said Lyles pulled a knife on two officers, who both shot her. The Seattle Times reported that one of the officers trained to use a taser, was not carrying it, a clear violation of the department's policy. Police officers should be a reflection of the society we live in, and I am starting to see what type of society we're living in. In the area of crime and justice there are no quick fixes, and there must be mechanisms in place to address such issues, but blatant disregard for the humane treatment of people caught on video should be enough for swift action even if it is the police that are the perpetrators.

When police are rogue and take a life, there are no excuses or mistakes that can be served to the people. Police should be justly prosecuted and put behind bars just as fast as black and brown people are unjustly arrested, charged, prosecuted, and sent to prison. In the last thirteen cases that were caught on video, outrage ensued, racial tensions were aroused, and protests erupted all across America. This was to no avail, as the police killings have not ceased. The only swift reaction was police departments and their officers offering excuses and explanations for their wrongful actions, despite clear-cut video evidence showing quite different versions of events. Many cases are clearly mishandled and are grossly unjustified. Police officers have been indicted in seven cases. In four of these, grand juries have declined to bring charges.

The police officers in all thirteen cases were placed on administrative leave or reassigned. Prosecutors are hesitant to prosecute the same police officers they deal with on a daily basis. There is a code of blue, which means departments and district attorneys protect their own. Facts given, jurors often find officers not guilty so they are also partly to blame. In most civil suits the police departments and cities rarely admit to wrongdoing. Almost all agreements state no admission of fault. The true oxymoron is many of the victim's families have been awarded settlements.

Samuel Dubose $4.85 million
Sandra Bland $1.9 million
Freddie Gray $6.4 million
Walter Scott $6.5 million
Tamir Rice $6 million
Laquan McDonald $5 million
Eric Garner $5.9 million

Settlements do not equate to police accountability. In many cities, settlements do not come out of the police department's budget. We can rest assured that police departments or cities do not give "pay-outs" (millions at that) unless it's felt they have not done right by the victim. Let's not be distracted by the smoke created by political pundits and the president. This is not only a Black Lives Matter issue but a human issue. Unarmed black and brown people are being killed by mostly white cops. I ask with an open heart, can you really be upset with those who choose to support or kneel for those who are no longer here? If you are unmoved by this, then ask yourself what if it were your immediate family member, relative or friend: would it matter then?

MASTER MANIPULATOR

"It is not as much as we are divided, it's we are disconnected." -unknown

As the NFL silently protested, pioneered by our beloved brother Colin Kaepernick the president of the United States dragged him into a debate that had seemed to be dying down, despite the attention around Kaepernick being "black balled." Trump did what Trump does best, ostracized the protest with his rhetoric.

@RealDonaldTrump

"Tremendous backlash against the NFL and its players for disrespect for our country. #standforouranthem"

@RealDonaldTrurnp
"The issue of kneeling has nothing to do with race. It is about respect for our country, flag and national anthem. NFL must respect this."

@RealDonaldTrurnp
"Very important that NFL players stand tomorrow and always, for playing of our national anthem. Respect our flag and our country!"

@RealDonaldTrump
"Sports fans should never condone players that do not stand proud for their Nations Anthem or their country. Change policy."

@RealDonaldTrump
"If a player wants the privilege of making millions of dollars in the NFL, or other leagues, he or she should not be allowed to disrespect our Great American Flag (or Country) and should stand for the National Anthem. If not, you're FIRED. Find something else to do."

@RealDonaldTrurnp
"Courageous patriots have fought and died for our

great American Flag. We must honor and respect it! Make America Great Again!"

These are the divisive tactics Trump chooses. Not once in his twitter rants did he mention the reason behind the NFL protest or how Kaepernick was advised by a veteran (Nate Boyer) that kneeling is more of a sign of respect than sitting. He also failed to mention that our military displays at NFL games were once financed by the government. This imagery of an organic, wholesome patriotism is fraudulent. Players standing for the anthem was never a tradition until they began using sports teams as a marketing ploy meant to sell manufactured patriotism.

Prior to 2009, nobody even realized it was a standard practice. In 2009 the NFL's policy changed from players standing to: "players being encouraged" to stand. The Department of Defense (D.O.D.) payed the NFL millions for things like flyovers, flag unfurlings, emotional color guard ceremonies, enlistment campaigns, and national anthem performances. In 2015 Arizona Sen (R) Jeff Flake and (R) John McCain revealed in a joint oversight report that nearly $5.4 million in taxpayer dollars has been paid out to 50 pro teams (14 NFL teams, NBA, NASCAR, MLB, and more). The report showed some teams were paid for anthem protests. These displays of paid patriotism were included within the $6.8 million that the D.O.D has spent on sports marketing contracts since the 2012 fiscal year.

The U.S flag codes are codes set in place so we do not disrespect our American flag in any way, form or fashion. The U.S. Flag Codes do not permit the manufacturing of the U.S flag; no miniature U.S. flags, buttons, hats, clothing, absolutely no manufacturing of our U.S. flag. The flag is not to be rolled out horizontally unless a flag is laid over a casket. To do any of these things is to disrespect the flag. Given the facts, the question must then be asked: should Kaepernick's stance (kneeling during the anthem) be condemned, or rather the government and the NFL for paid patriotism and neglect of the U.S. Flag Codes? To me, Kaepernick is the true patriot for using his constitutional right: freedom of speech.

CHAPTER 13

I AM MORE THAN JUST AN ATHLETE

"Commitment is a big part of what I am and what I believe. How committed are you to winning? How committed are you to being a good friend? To being trustworthy? To being successful? How committed are you to being a good father, a good teammate, a good role model? There's that moment every morning when you look in the mirror: Are you committed, or are you not?"

--Lebron "King" James

"Shut up and Dribble"

It is incumbent upon me that I truthfully inform the people that denouncement of systemic oppression has often spilled over to what many of us detest: the desecration of the American flag. Nevertheless, consolement can be found (for those who become outraged when they see or hear of the flag being desecrated) by simply considering America's ugly past.

As many Americans choose to exercise their right to free speech by indulging in acts that are abhorrent to others, we must respect their right to do so. The post Obama-present Trump era has caused an atmosphere of overt racism to spring up. I would say there are two perspectives to this dilemma: the unmasking of covert racism, which leads to the display of overt racism, and the empowerment of the people to speak, exposing covert racism that has attempted to hide behind our glorious flag.

Today we see social media (Twitter, Instagram, Facebook, etc.) being used to address social change through hashtags such as #metoo, #blacklivesmatter, #iammorethanjustanathlete, #takeaknee and other widespread movements, whose motives are to bring awareness to social issues that are affecting society. We also saw the display of overt racism in our society, as captured by the experience of Lebron James. In an "Uninterrupted" Uber ride special, with ESPN's Cari Champion and NBA star Kevin Durant, James tackled some very important social issues Champion eventually led the conversation towards president Trump, to which Lebron went on to say, "It's not even a surprise when he says something" Lebron continued, "It's laughable and it's scary." As the conversation progressed further, James delved into the incident when the gates of his home in Los Angeles were sprayed with a racial slur. "I'm a black man with a bunch of money living in Brentwood, California and having "NIGGER" spray-painted over my gate that lets you know I ain't too far removed and I still got a lot more work to do."

This teaches us that, no matter how far you've come, how much access or money you have, as an African American there will always be attempts to impress upon you that you are inferior. Lebron handled the situation with class and his words were well received because it was a humanizing moment to hear of such an incident reaching his doorsteps, so to speak. It highlighted the overt racism despite his global success. However, Lebron's outspoken personality did not go down well with everyone, case-in-point Laura Ingraham.

Laura Ingraham, a Fox news anchor, took issue with Mr. James's comments, saying, "I'm numb to this commentary like must they run their mouths like that? Unfortunately, a lot of kids, and some adults, take these ignorant comments seriously. Look, there might be a cautionary lesson in Lebron for kids: this is what happens when you attempt to leave high school early to join the NBA. And it's always unwise to seek political advice from someone who gets paid a hundred million dollars a year to bounce a ball. Oh, and Lebron and Kevin: you're great players but no one voted for you. Millions elected Trump to be the coach. So keep the political commentary to yourself or as someone once said, 'shut up and dribble.'"

Her words were not acceptable to the black community. Ingraham received just as much criticism as she dished out:

@DWADE
"They use to try and hide it... now the president has given everyone the courage to live their truths."

Draymond Green commented: "It just shows where we really are." Kevin Durant was asked in a recent interview with Sam Amick of USA Today, "Did you watch the whole segment?" Durant responded, "Yeah, I watched it. But like I said, you tend to focus on the positive. It's just sad to see people who think that way. It's weird. It's not even a place where we should be as humans. To me, it was racist. What does [skin color] have to do with anything? We all have an opinion just like she has an opinion that I disagree with. But I'm not going on T.V. tweeting and calling her..."

Ingraham's statements attempt to undermine athletes and who James really is as a human being; as if he is not intelligent enough as a black athlete to speak on social issues. She was stereotypical when stating that James didn't finish high school, which is false. Not only that, but one would think with her being a news reporter, she would vet her stories. Just in case she didn't know, James graduated from St. Vincent-St. Mary High School. He skipped college and entered the NBA. Ms. Ingraham was swift to condemn James but failed to condemn Joe the Plumber by telling him to shut up and fix things, or Kid Rock to shut up and entertain, or Clint Eastwood to shut up and act; but I guess she wouldn't, especially since their views, more or less, align with hers.

Though James is now an NBA superstar, he came from humble beginnings and has now built a team of sincere friends to help push forward his global brand.

James, Rich Paul, Maverick Carter, and Randy Mims are all childhood friends who formed an agent and sports company called LRMR. LRMR handles James' marketing, including the marketing of "The Decision." Despite criticism, James donated three million dollars to charity, with the majority of the money going to Boys' & Girls' Clubs around the country, and the remainder was distributed to charities that also cater to children. James is one of the most charitable amongst his peers, receiving the J. Walter Kennedy Citizen Award from the NBA for his "outstanding service and dedication to the community." James' upbringing is one of the reasons why he is so charitable. His business savvy has trickled over into sports by signing two-year deals with a one-year option, allowing the re-signing of new contracts after every season; capitalizing off the NBA's rising salary cap. Not bad for a so-called high school dropout.

In addition to all of this he, along with business partner Maverick Carter, owns a production company called "Spring Hill Entertainment," which recently announced the production of a new film in the "House Party" series that King James will have a cameo in.

James is more than just an athlete. He is a mentor, a father, and a global icon. He's also an active supporter of non-profit organizations such as "After School All Stars," which began as a Bike-a-thon, "Wheels for Education," which was developed to help at-risk youth in Akron, such as raising money for children's education by providing mentorships in the areas of reading and math and giving children a place to go after school. The ultimate agenda was to keep kids in school while discouraging them from dropping out before graduating.

Overall, James' foundation has handed out more than 40 million dollars to the program. Recently, James has opened his own school in partnership with the Akron board of education and teamed up with the University of Akron to provide scholarships to 1,100 kids. The children must participate in the program and parents are encouraged to participate as well. James is very involved and is connecting with these kids via social media while away. The first graduating class will be 2021. The scholarships cover over $9,500 of the students' annual tuition costs. Lebron hopes to extend the program throughout the state of Ohio. Another one of James' favorite charities is the Boys' & Girls' Club of America. While playing in Miami (for the Miami Heat) James and his wife donated and designed furniture, replaced roofs, and repaired children's workplaces. They donated 1,000 new computers to 59 Boys' & Girls' Clubs of America.

He joined Michael Jordan and Magic Johnson in donating to the "Muhammad Ali-A Force for Change," an exhibit that honors Ali's stellar boxing career and his social activism. James donated $2.5 million to that cause, stating, "Ali was an important inspiration to him as an athlete but also a change for justice."

James is also a major contributor to the "Children

Defense Fund," which in unison with one of his favorite non-profits OnexOne, has a program that focuses on "at risk" children who come from poor backgrounds and helps these children complete their education. Their mission includes five pillars: hunger, health, education, water and play. James possesses a humanitarian spirit and has never let his ego get in the way of him inspiring children and assisting them in ways he wasn't as a youth.

For those reasons (and many others) Ingraham's comments about James says more about her racist assumptions of him than about the actual facts in respect to this man, which can be seen in his response to her derogatory statements: "To be an African American kid and growing up in the inner city with a single parent mother and not being financially stable and to make it where I've made it to today, I think I've defeated the odds. I want every kid to know that, and I want everybody to know that the youth can do it as well. That's why I will not shut up and dribble. I mean too much to my two boys here, their best friend right here; my daughter at home, my wife, my family and all these kids who look up to me for inspiration in trying to find a way, and find some leeway on how they can become as great as they can be and now those dreams can become a reality."

James continued, "The best thing she did was help create more awareness. I appreciate her for giving me even more awareness. For me to be sitting here on the greatest weekend of the NBA, All-Star weekend... this is the best weekend in the NBA where all the countries in the whole entire world come watch the greatest players in the world no matter if they're a part of Thursday, Friday, Saturday or Sunday, and I get up here and talk about social injustice, equality, and why a woman on a certain network decided to tell me to shut up and dribble. So, thank you, whatever your name is. I get to talk about what's really important and how I can help change kids, not only in America, but in Brazil and England and Mexico and all over. So, thank you."

These guys (Lebron James, Kevin Durant, Stephen Curry, and others) come from these same situations that they are committed to changing and impacting. There's a sense of connection. Durant just dropped 10 million in partnership with Prince George County public schools to develop "college track." An after-school program that helps disadvantage kids get into college. The Washington Post reported that, the college track program is set to open later this year (2018) and will be the first of its kind on the east coast. The Durant Center will open in Seat Pleasant, his hometown, and will house the first of three college track facilities in the D.C. area

The 10-year program gives underprivileged students the tools they need to get into college: test prep, tutoring, and resources on how to get financial aid and into the right college. "We didn't have the resources to get our minds thinking on the next level," Durant said to the

Washington Post. "I want to do my part. Whatever it is, if college track students want to be the next Steve Jobs or the next influencer or the next tastemakers, they can get there." Kevin Durant's teammate Stephan Curry is assisting on the donation front. Curry, the leader of "Nothing but Nets" campaign, is using his long-range prowess, in partnership with the United Nations, to help take down malaria by aiming to bring protective nets to millions of people around the world who are prone to the mosquito-borne disease.

Now with all these contributions these players are attached to, no wonder Ingraham wants them to "shut up and dribble." For the youth today James, Durant, and Curry are more than just athletes, they will never stay silent, but will be loud with their actions and bold with their statements.

"I've always wanted to be more than just a boxer, more than the three-time heavy weight champion. I wanted to use my fame, and this face that everyone knows so well to help uplift and inspire people around the world."

-Muhammad Ali

Reaching Back

The current protest surrounding the NFL has sparked a national conversation, where the plight of minorities has taken center stage. Kaepernick has preferred to use his platform to address the ongoing systemic injustices prevalent in our society. Kaepernick's protest has also provided us an opportunity to look directly in the mirror and ask ourselves, "Am I doing enough?"

Many athletes seemed to have asked themselves that same question and have acted on the answer. This is evidenced by the many charitable contributions to numerous causes that lend credence to the fact that athletes have actually been reaching back. The things these athletes do outside of sports are life changing. Following are just some instances of the many athletes who reach back. Seattle Seahawks quarterback, Russell Wilson, is the national ambassador for the Charles Ray III Diabetes Association and he also raises money for charities through his "Invested with Russell" campaign. Russell Wilson also orchestrates the "Why not you" foundation, supporting various children's causes and spends a great deal of his free time visiting children at Seattle's Children's Hospital.

Let's go over on the defensive side of the ball and take a look at how Ndamukung Suh (who is one of the NFL's highest paid players) pitches in. Suh, once labeled in a negative light but never celebrated for his generosity, donated $2.6 million to the University of Nebraska and also donated $250,000 to his high school. It doesn't stop there for the big-hearted fellow. Suh owns the "Ndamukung Suh Foundation," which is geared towards helping children with school supplies, offering scholarships, and is committed to assisting athletic programs around the country. I challenge people to stop limiting these players to just their on-the-field performances.

There are those whose actions speak for themselves such as The NFL's 2016 Walter Payton Recipient, Anquan Boldin. Mr. Boldin and his wife, Donnie, have been heavily involved in their hometown Pahokee, FL. They have set the example for their two sons by way of their Anquan Boldin Foundation, which is expanding the educational and life opportunities to underprivileged children. Throughout the year they hold different events such as back-to-school giveaways, holiday shopping sprees, and annual Thanksgiving dinners. Anquan is also a big supporter of the Youth Football League. His "Q81" foundation seeks to put education of students first, and promote positive academic attitudes and behaviors while facilitating safe environments.

These athletes are very much connected to the same everyday issues as they are subject to experience the same situations that black men face every day. Whether it be by racial profiling, outright discrimination or an unlawful traffic stop, these men know the realities that people of color are subjected to, and some of these men have family members who have been directly affected by racism.

In 2015, Corey Jones (a cousin of Boldin) was shot to death by plain-clothes police officer in South Florida after Jones's car broke down on the side of the road. This tragic incident was a catalyst which eventually led Boldin to retiring after 14 seasons in the NFL. Boldin would express his sentiments for the cause in a statement to ESPN: "I feel drawn to make the larger fight for human rights." Boldin concluded by stating, "My life purpose is bigger than football." This ultimately led Boldin, Michael Jenkins, and other players to meet with politicians on Capitol Hill in 2016.

One of the most important things for me is that we feel like our voices are being heard. So, seeing those brothers in a Capitol Hill meeting and working towards change is tremendous. It shows that our cries and plea's don't just fall by the way side. Boldin echoed the same sentiments: "You want to make sure they understand the things that we, as the African American community, are going through. I don't think our community feels that way right now, especially when it comes to law enforcement and the way we're being policed." Anquan elaborated further, "Our neighborhoods are feeling hurt. Number two, you want to see change on policy, in terms of how we train our police officers. And lastly, you want accountability that justice will be served for all—make sure that the relationship between the African American community and police can be better. There's work to be done to prevent these situations." Boldin has dedicated his retirement towards reaching back and helping those in need, and working towards bridging the divide on both sides. I ask those who question brother Kaepernick's style of protest, instead shouldn't we be questioning ourselves for the attempt to find fault and dismiss the obvious truths in what the protest actually stands for.

Philadelphia Eagles Super Bowl champ, Malcolm Jenkins, has paired his protest with policy advocacy. Jenkins visited D.C. politicians to talk criminal justice reform, and met with Philadelphia's Caucus of Working Educators to discuss the Black Lives Matter movement. He took part in a ride-along with a Philadelphia police officer in order to get first-hand insight of working in law enforcement. Jenkins quickly began to realize how well-received he was and used his status to further his mission in endeavors that will effect real change in the community and society as a whole.

Recently, president Trump uninvited the Philadelphia Eagles from a scheduled celebration (for winning the Super Bowl.) Reporters bombarded Jenkins with questions in regards to Trump's decision. Instead of speaking to the media, Jenkins used signs, many of which consisted of written statistical facts. Reporters seemed more concerned with the president's antics than real systemic issues.

Reporters:

"Are you upset with the White House for canceling the event?

Malcom do you feel it was fair for the President to cancel the White House trip even though a large majority of the team wasn't going?"

Malcom answered the reporter's questions with signs that read:

"More than 60 percent of people in prisons are people of color."

"Nearly 200,000 juveniles enter the adult criminal system each year for non-violent crimes."

"Any given night, 500,000 sit in jail. Convicted? No. Too Poor? Yes."

"In 2018, 439 people shot and killed by police (thus far.)"

"In U.S. Pop 8% African American males - shot by police – 25% African American males."

One reporter had the nerve to ask "What does that have to do with the White House yesterday?"

Jenkins answers, seemingly ignored by reporters, prompting him to flash "YOU ARE NOT LISTENING." Jenkin's other signs displayed a sizeable list of NFL players, who he considered "true patriots," for their charitable work. Reaching back is an obligation, as seen in the examples of these men. It is obvious that these athletes will continue to speak up and protest on issues that are near and dear to us all.

I believe in a statement Boldin made about what football boils down to:

"Football in its purest form is what we all strive for as a nation. People from all different races, religions and backgrounds working together for one shared goal. The core values taught in football are some of the most important ones you learn in life. To always be there for the guy next to you and not let your fellow man down.

You do whatever it takes to make sure your brother is ok."

For society to vilify any man for wanting better or for doing better is the opposite of why these guys play as hard as they do and give back as much as they have. So, before we judge, let's first attempt to listen.

Actions speak louder than words... So, let's all start reaching back.

CHAPTER 14

Against All Odds!

"No one is going to give you the education you need to over throw them. Nobody is going to teach you your true history, teach you your true heroes if they know that knowledge will help set you free."

-Assata Shakur.

<u>Little Rock Nine</u>

On September 25, 1957 in Little Rock, Arkansas nine black students audaciously stepped foot into an all-white high school amid a hostile group of all-white students. These students became known as the Little Rock Nine. Prior to their step towards desegregation, The United States Supreme Court (1954) had handed down its historical ruling in <u>Brown vs. Board of Education</u>, which ordered school integration throughout the United States. Leading this charge and handpicking the nine students was NAACP President Daisy Gatson Bates.

The Little Rock Nine, Thelma Mothershed Wair, Jefferson Thomas, MinniJean Brown Trickey, Terrence Roberts, Gloria Ray Karlmark, Ernest Green, Elizabeth Eckford, Melba Pattillo Beals, and Carlotta Walls Lanier all endured physical abuse, verbal abuse, and harassment.

Minnijean Brown Trickey's mother was fired from her job for refusing to remove her daughter from the school, Minnijean was later expelled for retaliating after a group of girls threw a purse full of combination locks at her. Melba Pattillo had acid thrown in her face and Gloria Ray was pushed down a flight of stairs. These acts perpetrated against them solely for being black in America.

Though the threats were constant, the students continually attempted to complete a full day of school. With multiple unsuccessful attempts and the constant presence of violence, President Dwight Eisenhower, deployed 1,200 armed soldiers from the 101st Airborne to assist in keeping the peace. You would have to picture what the atmosphere was like to truly understand the work that was done. 1,200 armed soldiers for the protection of nine black students, now that was white outrage. At the culmination of this ordeal, the NAACP had to literally force the Federal Courts to order the integration at Little Rock Central High School.

What these nine iconic students did was truly amazing and paved the way for other schools to eventually integrate. Out of the Little Rock Nine, Ernest Green became the only student to graduate as the first African American with a diploma from Little Rock Central High, with the rest of the nine eventually receiving their diplomas through correspondence or other high schools. All of the students went on to do amazing things in life, like earning degrees and assisting presidents. Ernest Green worked under Jimmy Carter as his press secretary in the Department of Labor. Melba Patillo became a reporter for NBC and worked under President Clinton in the Department of Workforce Diversity.

In 1999, President Bill Clinton awarded the Little Rock Nine with the Congressional Gold Medal for their monumental role in the civil rights movement. 10 years later, our first black president, Barack Obama, invited them to his inauguration. The Little Rock Nine made it possible for the likes of Barack and Michelle Obama to attend schools such as Princeton and Harvard. What they endured also allowed schools in America to become the all-inclusive institutions in which their sacrifices were meant to be. It is in the spirit of the Little Rock Nine that Kaepernick endures, sacrifices, and sets the trend for the coming generation to stand, no matter the odds.

***

"I know now that the most damaging thing a people in a colonial situation can do is allow their children to attend any educational facility organized by the dominant enemy culture." George Jackson, Soledad Brother

Statistical and Educational Inequality

In the past, our ancestors never had the right to an education. "Being a fool is one of the basic ingredients of any incidents to the maintenance of the slavery system" (Lynch, 1712:1.) In order to continually subject our ancestors to slavery their right to an education was withdrawn and often slaves would be beaten if caught reading or writing. It was also once said "to keep information and knowledge away from black people put it in a book." Therefore, it should be at the forefront of our minds to fully educate ourselves and absorb as much knowledge, experience, and wisdom as possible. The stark reality for our community is that an increasing number of black children lack the same educational opportunities as their white counterparts; a large majority grows up in deprived economic environments and households. This often means that their levels of nutrition and health are considerably lower, in some cases parental educational achievements are significantly lower and there is more likely to be a history of parental interaction with the justice system. White parents often have higher educational expectations for their children than black parents. When considering all these factors, it is not surprising that black children lack positive attitudes with regards to education, set little to no personal goals on educational achievement, and rarely have conversations with their parents about their academic achievement or goals for the future.

When broadening the scope and looking at the issue from a wider perspective, we see in England a disproportionate number of black boys deemed low educational achievers and have higher rates of exclusion from school. As a direct result, they are almost more than likely to underachieve within the job market. U.K. statistics, circa 2015, relating to black males demonstrate low academic achievement, disproportionate unemployment, and over representation in the criminal justice system. Approximately 10% of prisoners within the United Kingdom are black. For black British males, this means they account for 49% of the ethnic minority in prison populations, despite only representing 2.8% of the country's population.

Sadly, the educational and judiciary systems in the U.K. mirror that of the United States, albeit on a smaller scale, because both are institutionally and systematically racist. Currently, there are more black juveniles incarcerated in America than attend college. It would appear that our education systems are a direct pipeline to our prison systems. We are failing our children from birth right up to adulthood. Within our community, the notion that we can achieve is almost non-existent. If we are to protect all individuals in their search for the enjoyment of life, then surely it should also include access to an education system that will educate all children, including and especially black children, to the highest standard.

As a teacher, I am all too aware that children are more receptive to education if they have the ability to relate to the topic and the teacher. I am not only able to impart my knowledge but learn from the children too, thus using their individual interests to link into the subject matter. For young black children, we need to recognize the value of learning about their history outside of the normal school curriculum. "A system of education is not one thing, nor does it have a single definite object, nor does it have a single definite subject, nor is it a mere matter of schools. Education is that whole system of human training within and without the school house walls, which molds and develops men," (W.E.B. Du Bois, 1903.)

Black history did not start with slavery, our history dates back centuries, yet within a school environment we are only ever portrayed as slaves. My job as a teacher while working in a predominantly black school, where the majority of the black students either came from one-parent families or from lower-income families, was to educate them in all aspects of life. It was not merely enough to teach them the curriculum but also to share knowledge of self and that despite our present circumstances we can achieve more and strive for better given the right tools, and sadly these tools are not always given to the children that need them the most. I strongly believe that education consists of a multitude of pedagogical tutelage and opportunities that when successfully combined will prepare children for their future. "Education is the development of power and ideal," (W.E.B. Du Bois.)

In the past within most communities, but especially within the black community, fathers were fathers to any number of children and would contribute in real ways and provide positive role models. Even children who had no father figure would have a male within the vicinity that would be there for them. Sadly, within today's society this is lacking with the increase in absent fathers, incarcerated fathers, and a general lack of family values and structure. The lack of role models leaves our young males with no input that can affect their lives in a productive and supportive manner. I have, however, been fortunate to witness the positive effects on black and brown children after having black and brown male teachers that could reach and relate to them. For them to have access to a positive black role model meant they were open to learning something different and to witness how a man can and should carry himself. For the lucky ones this was invaluable, however, it means that for a large proportion of young males, aspects of their education are unavailable when considering that only certain things can be passed on from man to boy. Single mothers of black boys can attest to the fact of how imperative it is for their children to have positive black role models within their lives in order to educate them on aspects of being a man that the mother will never be able to instill in them. If this is lacking during the formative years, then it can continue to yet another generation of boys who struggle to cope and adapt to the role of a black adult male.

***

Black and brown men like Kaepernick used their education to reach greater heights when their careers became derailed in a society that was designed for them to fail. Kaepernick is the kind of black man that helps to fill the void in the "black reality." Where we lack black men as role models in our immediate environments (or homes) we can direct our children to men such as him. The more men of his caliber that step up and place themselves in reach of the people and communities, the better off black and brown boys become.

Kaepernick has given us one more desperately-needed black man that young black and brown boys can look to for inspiration. In him, black and brown boys can see what society has been attempting to hide for far too long: That black men are intelligent. That black men do not have to entertain you to have worth. That black men do stand for principles and values. That black men have a moral conscience. That black men are not vicious or violent, but nevertheless are strong. Black men can move the people by what's just and equal for all; even in a society that has attempted to crush them for hundreds of years.

"Stand up, black man! Our children await... education is our key, may we open the doors!" (Authors, 2018.

CHAPTER 15

Sportsmanlike Conduct

"The ultimate measure of a man is not where he stands in moments of comfort and convenience, but where he stands at times of challenge and controversy."

-Martin Luther King, Jr.

Mahmoud Abdul-Rauf

Sports is a universal activity that brings together different races, religions, and creeds. In a testosterone-filled atmosphere hyped with masculinity and femininity during which time nothing else matters except the team you're rooting for. Strangers form alliances, share intimacies (hugs, fist-bumps, and handshakes) cheer and root together. As black and brown people break barriers in sports, it has forced white America to address a never-ending problem: that black Americans would not only be compensated well but given the same stage to share as their white counterparts.

How you handle your position means a lot. That's why Kaepernick is admired by many, for choosing to use his stage and platform for something bigger than himself. Despite all opposition he stood upright and what shone forth was not fear in losing his career, but rather a legacy with no meaning and not having fulfilled his purpose.

We often look at public figures (i.e. artists, athletes, entertainers) and label them by their professions. But there comes a time when, eventually, profession and passion separates (unless of course, your profession is your only passion.)

This leads us to a very fine brother. Mahmoud Abdul-Rauf, a man who in 1996 caused us to have a real conversation. Born Chris Wayne Jackson, in Gulfport, Mississippi, to Mrs. Jacqueline Jackson, Chris converted to Islam and became known as Mahmoud Abdul-Rauf. Rauf, along with his two brothers, Dave and Omar, were raised in poverty (not an uncommon occurrence for black and brown people in America.) Rauf was diagnosed with "Tourette's Syndrome," which caused him to be placed in special education classes. Despite the obstacles Rauf would flourish, especially on the basketball court. Averaging 29 points and 5.7 assists per game, he was invited to the McDonald's All-American Game and named Mississippi "Mr. Basketball" twice (1987-88.)

While attending college at the age of 24, Rauf was inspired after reading the autobiography of Malcolm X. In 1993, Rauf converted to Islam and while playing in the NBA became best known for the controversy created when he refused to stand for the national anthem. Ringing loud must have been the words of Malcolm X: "You're not so blind with patriotism that you can't face reality. Wrong is wrong, no matter who does it or says it.

Nobody can give you freedom, nobody can give you equality or justice against the oppressor. Truth is on the side of the oppressed today. It's against the oppressor, you don't need anything else." To me, it seems that Rauf had begun to contemplate that reality Malcolm had spoken of.

The Denver Nuggets selected Rauf with the third selection in the 1990 NBA Draft. His first year in the NBA he made the "All-Rookie" team. Abdul-Rauf led the league in free-throw percentages from the 1993-96 seasons. In '93, he won the "Most Improved Award." After the 1992-93 season, Abdul-Rauf signed a five year $13-million-dollar contract and led his team in scoring. Abdul-Rauf was also immaculate from the free-throw line, leading all players. As I baffled over what could lead a man, in 1996, to decide he would no longer stand for the national anthem, I began to search for what transpired in '96 or leading up to '96 that would cause a person to protest the national anthem. I was amazed to find not only one, but numerous incidents. For me, the question then became, when were there not issues or incidents affecting people of color? Of course, the answer was simply: there was no such time.

On March 10, 1996 Mahmoud Abdul-Rauf caused us to have a serious conversation when he sat down in the middle of the recital of the national anthem. When reporters questioned him after the game, he responded that he considered the flag "A symbol of oppression, of tyranny." He further stated, "I am a Muslim first, a Muslim last, and my duty is to my creator not to nationalistic ideology." The NBA suspended him without pay, citing a rule that requires players, coaches, and trainers to "stand in a dignified posture during the U.S. and Canadian Anthems. Within a day's time, the league withdrew the suspension and came to an agreement he would not sit, but stand while holding his hands into a posture of prayer. Just as Kaepernick's protest went on to spark a national debate, so did Abdul-Rauf's.

The sentiments still have not changed for those that oppose people from exercising their First Amendment rights, when it comes to standing for the national anthem. Abdul-Rauf was called a traitor and told to go to another country that does not enjoy the freedoms that we do, and he was booed on many occasions. During the rest of Abdul-Rauf's career he remained under scrutiny, which ultimately led him overseas to play for various international clubs.

If I must be blunt, a person of color has never had any reason to stand for the national anthem, considering its racist content. Standing is usually done out of respect and tradition. The flag is a symbol of oppression, and that oppression includes the enslavement of people of color for the purposes of someone else's bottom line. One of the reasons the United States has become one of the biggest powers in the world is because they had free slave labor to help build this country. Without such free labor, there would be no America.

We were trained to pledge allegiance to the flag of the United States of America from preschool on. Remember those recitals: "I pledge allegiance to the flag..." You never questioned why or what those words you were repeating really meant. To add more context as to why the pledge of allegiance was never meant to represent or include black and brown people, it is no secret who was considered 3/5 of a person in this country at the time of its inception.

I live with the fact that my country has killed, maimed, hung, whipped, burnt, shot, and still continues to murder unarmed black men and women of color with impunity. Then who should my allegiance be with when my own country is against me? Yes, as an African American I remain confused. And as people of color we still search for an answer. According to United States Supreme Court precedent:

Dred Scott vs. Sanford, 19 Howard (60 U.S.) 393 (1857) was one of the Supreme Court's most important slavery-related decisions in the history of the Court's existence. In a 7 to 2 majority, Chief Justice Roger Taney reached a three-part major conclusion that shook the nation's politics. These conclusions deeply affected the rights of blacks, free blacks in particular. 1) Blacks, even free blacks in the North, could never be considered citizens of the United States and could not sue in federal court as citizens of the states in which they lived. 2) The ban on slavery in the western territories that was part of the Missouri Compromise was unconstitutional because Congress had no power to regulate the territories beyond the Minimal Congress nor the territorial government. 3) Neither Congress nor the territorial governments could ever prohibit slaveholding in the western territories nor ban slavery through popular sovereignty.

What is equally important to consider as we come to terms with the racist tendencies of America is that the Dred Scott decision essentially ruled that blacks (people of color) as descendants of slaves, are not included, nor were they intended to be included, under the word 'citizen' in the Constitution; and therefore claim none of the rights and privileges which the instruments of legalities provide and secure to citizens of the United States. We must keep in mind that these were the sentiments of a chief "justice." Then we should have no issue with those who believe they receive no "justice" or "liberty" under the flag, thus they refuse to stand for the flag.

Twenty years after Mahmoud Abdul-Rauf decided to take a stand against the national anthem, Kaepernick refused to stand in 2016. Although these events span two different eras, the facts still remain unchanged. The generational cycle of oppression is still felt by those living in this reality. Whether it be sports figures with wide platforms because of their greatness or whether it be those unfortunate circumstances that befall black and brown people in America on a daily basis, the crimes of oppression continue to be exposed.

Syracuse 8

The discrimination of yesterday is still prevalent today, albeit in different forms. To date, discrimination is still as relevant as it was in the 50's, 60's, and 70's. Over the decades many demonstrations have taken place on college campuses around the nation as discrimination, inequality and unequal treatment of black and brown students has continued unabated in the arena of higher learning in America. The historical underpinnings associated with discrimination in our institutions of higher learning can be attested to by the account of the Syracuse 8.

In 1970, 9 Syracuse players (all of whom were African American) boycotted the 1970 football season in a demand for better treatment and to promote racial equality. Although dubbed "Syracuse 8," there were actually nine: Gregory Allen, Richard Bulls, John Godbolt, Dana Harrell, John Lobon, Clearence "Bucky" McGill, Alif Muhammad, Duane Walker, and Ron Womack. These students threw away the idea of individualism and brought into existence collectivism. They protested collectively because they weren't given the same treatment (medical and otherwise) and began to promote racial equality across the board in regards to the treatment suffered at the University.

In protesting, they were seeking strong academic support for black student athletes, fair competition for starting positions, and racial integration on the football coaching staff. Their protest actually started in the spring of 1969, with the black players accusing Coach Floyd "Ben" Schwartzwalder of discriminatory practices. The season opener later infused Syracuse's biggest campus riot. A pregame confrontation with 400 students and 100 cops, led to· the hurling of rocks, bottles, and wood; the spraying of gas; and use of excessive force by the police. Later that year, Syracuse's Chancellor, Corbally Jr, finally intervened and commissioned an investigation. Subsequently, a 600-page commission report concluded that the players' claims were justified.

Just as the "Syracuse 8" players protested and sacrificed their collegiate football career, as Kaepernick sacrificed his NFL football career in order to stimulate change and awareness. There is no difference in what they did and what Kaepernick is doing today, just different circumstances. For their courageous stance on the football field against discrimination and inequality they were honored 36 years later in 2006 with their SU letterman jackets that they received during their boycott. These players are shining examples for the change that Kaepernick kneels for.

MLB (Major League Baseball)

Steven A. Smith once commented on First Take: "When you're white, your talents are exploited all the way until the wheels fall off but when you're black there's a need to control you." Major League Baseball was once a white-dominated sport, but greatness is hard to overlook.

Jackie Robinson open the flood gates for people of color in the Major Leagues. He used his talents to push civil rights further which ultimately led him to paving the way for others and becoming a First Ballot (African American) Hall of Famer. If baseball could accept an African American, then why not America?

Robinson endured many acts of hate, racism, discrimination, and bigotry. This was a man who was spat upon, threatened with death, harassed in cities and towns across America, and even court martialed for refusing to sit in the back of the bus. Despite it all, he continued knowing his purpose was to sacrifice for the greater good, equality, and justice in America. He understood that being subjected to all the racism when he entered those white lines of the batter's box awaiting his first pitch was for a greater cause.

"Life is not important except the impact that it makes on lives." Robinson not only uttered those words, but he coined it in his journey. He had to discipline himself because of the challenging experience ahead. Jackie saw firsthand the raw emotions of white America while attempting to break the social barrier of being a black man in a white sport.

"I cannot stand and sing the anthem. I cannot salute a flag. I know I am a black man in a white world."

--Jackie Robinson

There was no better man to make this statement than a man who has traveled around America and despite his accomplishments in sports was consistently rejected by America based on his race.

Even today, such despicability remains in our society. Though there has been the attempt to hide racism, of late we've seen a display of overt racism, as some are still convinced that white comfort means more than black lives. We would never have known of the outrage and hate of former L.A. Clippers (NBA) owner Donald Sterling if not for a recently released recording. People of color were good enough to play for his team, coach his team, and support his tea, but the one thing that outraged him was a black man merely sitting next to his girlfriend.

The Oakland A's Bruce Maxwell decided he was not going to be on the wrong side of history. Maxwell was the first MLB player to kneel. Maxwell explained his reasoning. "I'm going to continue to do it. This isn't a one-day thing. If things really don't change, I'll roll into next season. This is an ongoing issue. This is happening across the country. It might take a few more people. It might take a little while. Racism has been going on since this country was founded. But stepping up and recognizing the fact that people in this country fought so I could do this."

Maxwell tweeted @Bruu_Truu13
"This now has gone from Black Lives Matter topic to just complete inequality of any man and woman that wants to stand for right!"

Bruce Maxwell comes from a military background so there is no disrespect when he kneels during the Anthem. He understands those who served or are serving have fought for rights such as free speech. The Oakland A's tweeted, "We respect and support all our players' constitutional rights and freedom of expression." The NFL and its owners should take a page out of the Oakland A's playbook. Players must understand: an attack on one is an attack on all. There is an importance for players of all sports to show solidarity, as more is accomplished when there is a show of unity.

I recall the New England Patriots quarterback Tom Brady's "deflate-gate" scandal, and the widespread support he received from players. Quarterbacks from several teams even came out saying they had deflated footballs to fit their hand size as well during their careers. I wonder why we hear no such support from fellow Quarterbacks on Kaepernick's unemployment the way

Maxwell and other sports figures have. As there were other greats in their respective sports who paved the way, and spoke up for civil rights and against injustice. To speak up is to exercise your right to free speech and to say to those who oppose: "Our voices will not be silenced."

***

"Next to God we are indebted to women, first for life itself, and then for making it worth living."

--Mary McLeod Bethune

<u>Howard University</u>

Throughout history, women have been at the forefront of our struggle and played pivotal roles. Women such as Rosa Parks, Angela Davis, Florynce Kennedy, Kathleen Cleaver, Kimberle Williams Crenshaw, Assata Shakur, Elaine Brown, Chaka Khan, Tarika Matilaba, Alice Walker, Shirley Chisolm, Charlene A. Carruthers, Jessica Byrd, Alicia Garza, Patrisse Cullars, and Opal Tometi have been very vocal and active in promoting equality and raising awareness on the issues prevalent to black people. Without women's contributions, we would not have achieved the milestones that we've reached at various junctures throughout history. That's why there's no surprise but true honor and delight to see women emerge in the protest of resistance.

213

At a Howard University home game, not far from the White House, the announcer says, "We ask that you please rise as we honor the United States of America." In the middle of the field the JROTC presents colors and the band plays the Star-Spangled Banner. The cheerleaders courageously opted to kneel.

The cheerleaders' protest began in September 2016, shortly after Kaepernick's protest gained national attention. Sydney Stallworth, one of the team's captains said, "I think of the national anthem and what it stands for, I think about liberty and justice for all and how it's not being executed in our country right now. And I think about how lucky I am to go to the best historically black university in the country not arguably; it's the greatest and I'm so lucky to have this platform."

Howard University cheerleaders elected to protest on their own. For decades at home games the anthem has been paired with "Lift Every Voice and Sing" which has come to be known as the black national anthem and has been traditionally played before the Star-Spangled Banner. The Howard cheerleaders, band dancers, and some spectators raised their fists in the black power salute. In a choreographic manner, the cheerleaders kneeled one by one in protest to the playing of the Star-Spangled Banner.

The same day at Kennesaw state, a public university in Georgia, five cheerleaders where threatened for similar protests. In regard to the students' protest, Marc

Lamont Hill (professor at Temple University who studies African culture) put it in perspective: "It is not surprising that when there's an anthem protest you see H.B.C.U.'s at the forefront of the resistance, because that's where we've always been. HBCU's are a space of nature. Where you can be surround by black genius, and black excellence can be normalized."

Demarco Brooks, who became the cheerleader's coach that season said he opposed kneeling, "It wouldn't have been my first choice," but he respected their rights. He decided that each cheerleader decides whether to kneel or not. Camille Washington, the mother of a Howard player was in attendance and wore a Kaepernick 49ers jersey in support of his protest. Ms. Washington stated that: "I'm a teacher and I want our kids to know they have a voice, and one way to do that is protesting in a way that brings light to what they believe in. In a country where you have rights and a Constitution that backs your rights, your rights should not be silenced."

"Injustice is still continuing," Stallworth said. "So, were going to continue to kneel until we see change."

CHAPTER 16

History Repeats Itself

"Those who do not learn from history are doomed to repeat it. This is why blacks have repetitive setbacks. Because we don't learn from history."

--Rudolph R. Windsor

Throughout history, people of color have always rebelled against the American flag, Constitution, and mindset. This rebellion has never been without cause or premise, nor has it abated in these modern times. As a nation built on the backs of slaves, after the near annihilation of the land's natives, should we wonder why the people would rebel against those ideals which, to this very day, seem hypocritical?

In 2001, black democratic Tennessee State Representative Henri Brooks, chose not to stand while her colleagues were reciting the Pledge of Allegiance at the state capital in Nashville. Suggesting that the flag is a symbol of slavery and racial oppression, Brooks explained that she usually stands out of respect to her colleagues, but in her nine years she has not recited the Pledge of Allegiance: "It's not one nation under God and it's not liberty and justice for all," Brooks told the

Washington Post.

Brooks' sentiments were noted nearly twenty years prior to Kaepernick's stance. Besides the gap in time, the only significant difference (between the two controversies) is the notoriety surrounding the two situations. Indeed, Kaepernick's stage is bigger, technology now allows a broader audience and information is distributed faster in today's age. That said, the conditions which caused their respective stances have surely not changed.

What Brooks' and Kaepernick's stances do have in common is the criticism that they would receive. When Kaepernick stated: "I am not going to stand up to show pride in a flag for a country that oppresses black people and people of color," it was strikingly reminiscent to the statement "This flag represents the former colonies that enslaved our ancestors, and when this flag was designed, they did not have [black people] in mind," made by Mrs. Brooks in 2001. And surely they are not the only ones who share these sentiments in light of the evidence America has provided us with.

Of course, some were outraged at Brooks' stance just as many are outraged by Kaepernick's. But I ask, would these same outraged individuals remain outraged if they were provided with the facts and history which propel individuals to act just as Brooks and Kaepernick acted? Syndicated columnist, Julianns Malveaux, in coming to Brooks' defense asked (rhetorically) "with liberty for whom? And what is justice? For whom?" in reference to the pledge, the words of the pledge are "ridiculous." In terms of blacks having faith in the true meaning of the words at the time of their inception, its (the pledge) being "nothing but a lie, just a lie" Miss Malveaux would go on to inform FOX News in an interview related to Brooks' (2001) position.

The furor caused by Rep Brooks' stance culminated into conflict between herself and fellow democrats. In particular, State House Speaker Jimmy Naifeh, had the audacity to not only question Ms. Brooks, but also "requested" that she "wait outside" the House Chamber until the recital was finished. Are not citizens afforded the right to point out hypocrisy and hate regardless of where they attempt to hide? In typical fashion (supremacy) Naifeh attempted to intimidate Brooks with "patriotic aggression." "He approached me in a master-slave type manner," said Brooks, causing her to file a complaint with the ACLU for the infringement upon her First Amendment rights. It is always this aggression (rage) that causes the acts of violence (police killings) that we are witnessing on a nearly bi-monthly basis. When (some) whites have positions of authority they feel as if they have the right to demand that people of color bow to their every command and desire, and if refused, abuse ensues whether physical (the "whip" syndrome) or verbal (the attempt to degrade as "less than.")

Brooks chose to speak up, she refused to stand or

recite. A right earned by the blood, sweat, and tears of her ancestors. Who can deny that fact? Prior to Brooks' refusal, she had already been active in pushing back against institutional/systemic racism. Sponsoring legislation against racial profiling by police, seeking reparations for descendants of slaves, highlighting poverty, discrimination, and inequality. Brooks was making a statement as to a reality, affecting people of color in America. Her stance was in no regard some "knee jerk" reaction to some isolated occurrence, as she stated loud and clear: "pledging allegiance to the flag, to me is very hypocritical," in light of the facts which substantiate an ongoing effort to subjugate black and brown people in America by means of racist social control. In light of this, we can understand why Brooks would use her stage to confront the hypocritical act of pledging while many in society are being oppressed under the guise of "liberty and justice for all."

Kaepernick follows in the footsteps of many, known and unknown. The reality is that he has "grabbed the torch," thus there is a long line of incidents that correlate to his having a seat, taking a knee, and raising a fist in resisting the continuous and ongoing oppression in modern day America. The master-slave mentality described by Brooks has not ceased to exist in our society. As NFL owners have echoed Mr. Jimmy Neifel by giving ultimatums, and more importantly to notice, ordering by way of "policy" that NFL players remain in the locker rooms ("outside" as in the case of Brooks) while the hypocrisy is "recited" on the field.

As NFL approved a new on-field "National Anthem Policy" (2018) players are required to stand if they are on the field or remain in the locker room if they prefer. The policy subjects teams to fines if a player or any other personnel do not show respect for the anthem. Teams will also have the option to fine any player or personnel for any violation of the policy. This decision drew sharp responses from players. Torrie Smith of the Carolina Panthers tweeted: "Appropriate respect for the flag and anthem' implies that guys were being disrespectful towards it. Which is an opinion. Most people who believe that ignore the responses from the players and more importantly why men chose to protest." Demaurice Smith, executive director of NFLPA, tweeted: "History has taught us both patriotism and protest are like water; if the force is strong enough it cannot be suppressed. Today the CEO's of the NFL created a rule that people who hate autocracies should reject." He also tweeted: "Management has chosen to squash the same freedom of speech that protects someone who wants to salute the flag in effort to prevent someone who does not wish to do so."

The decision made by NFL owners was not "collective bargaining," but a unilateral decision made by the owners, ironfisted strongmen. The NFL's Players Association and its players were excluded from this matter. There is no true display of patriotism when one is forced by policy or rule to comply (standing in a dignified manner.) Now that this rule has been adopted, it ensures nothing but a meaningless and false show of nationalism and patriotism, while the real issues remain unresolved.

As we have witnessed Kaepernick take a stand in refusing to falsely portray the so-called ideals of the national anthem being upheld within our society, so too did Brooks, twenty years earlier, refuse to falsely imply the same in regards to the Pledge of Allegiance, a true example that history repeats itself.

CHAPTER 17

Muhammad Ali and Colin Kaepernick: Side by Side

"Every fruit has a seed in it that reproduces itself."

-Brother Darrell Muhammed (N.O.I.)

Every era has their hero and every era has their king. Very few are generational heroes and that's exactly who Muhammad Ali is to black and brown people across the world. To put this in proper perspective, we must not compare our idols to each other for several reasons. For one, they are not in competition with each other. And two, it may be extremely difficult to compare an era in which one person lived to another.

What is comparable in terms of similarities is the impact and significance one has indented on history. Each generation differs, and to be generational is to have a lasting effect.

Muhammad Ali's actions (refusing draft) at the time; amid the heightened civil rights era, facing possible prison time, his boxing license suspended and stripped of his title, those had a major and lasting impact. We can find similarities in Kaepernick's stance and protest for this generation and century. I know in hindsight many will look at his stance and see the significance to Ali. Nelson Mandela graciously spoke these words: "Bear in mind our greatest glory is not in never falling, but rising every time you fall." To America, Ali was the symbol of resistance. No sports figure has ever been so outspoken and articulate with words than the "people's champ" Muhammad Ali. Ali was the first black male athlete to break down a lot of barriers in sports for people of color. When you see the Mayweather's of today, the LeBron's and the Richard Sherman's, you see Muhammad Ali.

The Resistance:

On April 28, 1967 Ali appeared in Houston, TX for his scheduled induction into the army. They were in for a rude awakening. Ali refused three times to step forward when his name was called. An officer warned him that by not stepping forward he was committing a felony punishable by five years in prison and a fine of $10,000. Ali stood fast in his refusal to answer or step forward and was eventually arrested. The same day, New York State Athletic Commission swiftly suspended his boxing title, with other commissions following suit. Ali was now officially "blackballed," stripped of his passport, and denied a boxing license in every state in America.

Ali went to trial on June 20th that same year, and the jury, after 21 minutes of deliberation found Ali guilty. Ali's legal team appealed the decision, which enabled him to remain free but still unable to either leave the country or box. The decision was eventually reviewed by the United States Supreme Court of 1971.

The Impact:

Clay vs. United States

"War is against the teachings of the Qur'an. I'm not trying to dodge the draft. We are not supposed to take part in no wars unless declared by Allah or The Messenger. We don't take part in Christian wars or wars of any unbelievers."

-Muhammad Ali

Ali spoke these words in regard to refusing the draft. As criticism grew Ali was called a traitor, had his home threatened, and was even shot at. Ali elaborated on his protest against the war: "Why should they ask me to put on a uniform and go ten thousand miles from home and drop bombs on brown people in Vietnam while so-called negro people in Louisville are treated like dogs and denied simple human rights? Ali was stripped of some of the most prime years (25-29) of his career for taking such a stance. As the civil rights movement garnered momentum, so did public opinion. At this time multiple activist began speaking out against the Vietnam War, including Ali, and public opinion began to sway.

Ali began touring the country, holding speaking

engagements at historical black colleges and universities across the nation. Ali's bravery inspired countless black Americans and others. Kareem Abdul Jabbar said in regard to Ali's anti-war position: "I remember the teachers at my high school didn't like Ali because he was so anti-establishment and he kind of thumbed his nose at authority and got away with it. The fact he was proud to be a black man and that he has so much talent... made some people think he was dangerous, but for those very reasons I enjoyed him." Rightfully so, Ali empowered countless others. When a person protests it is usually on behalf of the master more so for those who have yet to come to be able to reap the benefits of the sacrifice.

Al Sharpton spoke on Ali's bravery at the time and said "For the heavyweight champion of the world, who had achieved the highest level of athletic celebrity, to put all of that on the line: the money, the endorsements to sacrifice all of that for a cause, gave a whole sense of legitimacy to the movement and the causes with young people that nothing else could have done. Even those assassinated certainly lost their lives but they didn't voluntarily do that. He knew he was going to jail and did it anyway. That's another level of leadership and sacrifice."

The New York Times Columnist Rhoden wrote: "Ali's actions changed my standard of what constituted an athlete's greatness. Possessing a killer jump shot or the ability to stop on a dime was no longer enough. What were you doing for the liberation of your people? What were you doing for your Country, living up to the covenant of its founding principles? The principles of this country are what Mr. Ali challenged. We as American citizens are given freedom and liberty. With that liberty and freedom, we must challenge America's core values in order to test its foundation. No foundation is solidified if it has not been tested to make sure it's sturdy enough to pressure or build upon. That's exactly what we do every time we exercise our rights, we are testing the foundation in which the constitution was written. If it shakes, we fix (make amendments) in order to keep building."

On June 28, 1971 the U.S. Supreme Court overturned Ali's conviction by a unanimous 8-0 decision. The U.S. Supreme Court forced the New York State Boxing Commission to reinstate Ali's license.

The Legacy:

"The circumstances that surround a man's life are not important, how that man responds to those circumstances is important, his response is the determining factor between success and failure."

-Booker T. Washington

I quoted Booker T. Washington because it was befitting in reference to Ali's legacy. Cassius Clay dropped his slave name and took on a name that was befitting of the person he is: Muhammad (one worthy of praise) Ali (most high) and cemented his legacy by refusing to join the fight in the Vietnam War and standing up for black and brown people everywhere. Once highly criticized, now renowned and glorified, Ali was finally validated and vindicated. As America began the process of self-reflection and self-analysis, we began to see Ali was one who should be celebrated for tenacity, patience, and courage. Ali did what most were afraid to do: stand up.

Ali's celebration spread like wildfire, his hometown Louisville, Kentucky voted to change Walnut Street and rename it Muhammad Ali Boulevard. He was displayed on multiple magazine covers. Ali was named one of the 100 Most Important People of the Century by Time Magazine, named Sports Personality of the Century by Sports Illustrated and a BBC poll. Americans finally began to give Ali the accolades he deserved.

The praise didn't stop there; President Clinton presented Muhammad Ali with the Presidential Citizen Medal in 2001. The following president, Bush, also presented Ali with an award. In 2005 he received the Presidential Medal of Freedom. He also received the Otto Hahn Peace Medal in Gold from the UN association of Germany (DGVN) in Berlin for his works with the civil rights movements. Even shopping malls were named after Ali (Ali Mall.) Most importantly, a $60 million non-profit organization was named in his honor, The

Muhammad Ali Center, which opened in downtown Louisville. This center would assist in carrying on his legacy, the center celebrated Ali in two parts: the displaying of his boxing memorabilia and his boxing legacy. The second part focused on his social causes centered on core themes of peace, social responsibility, and growth. If we do not record accounts of history or display our history, it will become "his-story" to change, dilute and misconstrue as he sees fit.

Ali received praise and accolades within many different fields, with him being a man of many talents. University of Princeton presented Ali with an Honorary Doctorate of Humanities. He received Grammy nominations: One for his album of spoken word "I Am the Greatest," another for the best recording for children with his 1976 spoken-word novelty-record "The adventures of Ali and his Gang vs. Mr. Tooth Decay."

Ali became synonymous with the anti-war effort, for many he was boxing for an end to the bombing in Vietnam, the abolishment of the draft, and the reversal of a foreign policy that sought to impose American will abroad. Today he's remembered as a hero. Ali was a symbol of hope and change. The biggest change came in 1999, when the Muhammad Ali Boxing Reform Act was introduced and passed in 2000 to protect the rights and welfare of boxers in the United States. In May 2016, a bill was introduced to congress by Mark Wayne Mullin, a politician and former MMA fighter, to extend the Ali act to mixed martial arts. In June 2016, U.S Senator Rand Paul proposed an amendment to the U.S. Draft laws, a proposal to eliminate selective service.

In the end, Ali was the winner through it all. Throughout all uncertainty, will he fight again? Will he go to jail? Will he ever get his title back? All things unknown and all things considered, Ali stood fast. Never wavering, he changed minds, lives, perspectives, and sports. He rewrote history. Muhammad Ali will forever be the people's champ.

Muhammad Ali inspired the World.

***

Who would have thought that the 1968 Summer Olympics at Olympic Stadium in Mexico City would have a major impact in today's time? There have been many Olympics but this one would be historic. The three 200-meter race winners: U.S Athlete Tommie Smith, Australia's Peter Norman, and U.S athlete John Carlos, who finished 1st, 2nd, and 3rd respectively decided that they would speak for the unspoken and unheard cries around the world.

As they headed to the podium for their medals, two of the athletes· received their medals shoeless but wearing black socks, to represent black poverty. Smith wore a black scarf around his neck, representing black pride. Carlos unzipped his tracksuit top to show solidarity with all blue-collar workers in the U.S and wore a necklace of beads he described "were for those individuals that were lynched or killed and that no one said a prayer for, that were hung and tarred. It was for those thrown off the side of the boats in the middle passage." All three wore "Olympic Project for Human Right" badges as Norman joined them in solidarity. The inspiration came from Sociologist Harry Edwards, the founder of "OPHR" and his admiration of black athletes to boycott the games.

When the Star-Spangled Banner was played, Smith and Carlos delivered their salute with heads down. The Black Power Salute drew boos from the crowd and made news everywhere.

"If I win, I am American, not black American, but if I did something bad then they would say I am a Negro. We are black and proud of being black. Black America will understand what we did tonight."

-John Carlos

This whole protest was a silent protest, and in order to affect a greater and lasting impact, these three men used symbolism. Every defiant act was attached a symbol representing something meaningful. The "Black Power Salute" was giving power to the people and is still considered the symbol which unites the people in a common cause.

Today, Kaepernick has utilized the same style of

protest that symbol (taking a knee) represents.

Years after the Star Olympic Athletes silently
protested, Mr. Tommie was quoted as saying: "We are
concerned about the lack of the black assistant coaches.
About Muhammad Ali being stripped of his tittle, about
the lack of access to good housing and our kids not being
able to attend the top colleges." Kaepernick is now
carrying that torch for freedom, justice, and equality. No
one can tell him not to speak out against injustice and
inequalities. Throughout history a spokesman always
rose from amongst the people.

***

The Resistance:
The national anthem played...

In a preseason game against the Houston Texans,
Colin Kaepernick, 28 at the time, quietly took a seat on
the bench. It took the media two weeks before they took
notice or asked him why he was sitting during the
national anthem. Kaepernick's explanation when asked
was that he was making a statement about inequality,
injustice, and discrimination in this country. "I am not
going to stand up to show pride in a flag for a country

that oppresses black people and people of color," Kaepernick explained after the interview.

Kaepernick also explained how deep his sentiments ran: "To me, this is bigger than football and it would be selfish on my part to look the other way." He added he would continue to sit during the national anthem until he began seeing "significant change" for minorities. "They are bodies in the street," Colin said, "and people getting paid leave to get away with murder." As time progressed Kaepernick's words and protest have been misconstrued, misinterpreted, and simply misplaced.

After the killing of Alton Sterling, in Eric Reid's (Colin's teammate's) hometown of Baton Rouge, Reid's faith moved him to join Kaepernick's protest *.

*soon after Reid began joining Kaepernick in protesting he also found himself without a job in the NFL. He subsequently filed a collusion suit against the NFL while a free agent. At the time of the release of this book Reid's collusion case was pending, but he eventually signed a one year deal with the Carolina Panthers (September/October 2018) where he is now employed with that team.

Prior to the start of the NFL 2016 regular season, Nate Boyer (retired Green Beret) wrote an open letter to Kaepernick, which led to a meeting with Kaepernick and Reid, which then led to them having a dialogue on their protest and the manner in which they chose to protest. Kaepernick and Reid, after meeting with Boyer, adopted a new but well-known gesture: taking a knee. Nate Boyer changed these brothers' minds. Boyer had had a brief stint in the NFL

Reminiscing, Boyer thought of that one time when he ran out of the tunnel holding the American flag. Standing for the Anthem, he immediately thought of his sacrifices and the men he fought alongside that didn't make it back. Boyer thought of troops currently overseas and thought if he noticed a teammate sitting on the bench, how that would hurt him. Boyer didn't have any issues with why they were protesting, just the manner in which they chose. He felt sitting would be viewed as disrespect but changing the gesture would be more respectful.

Reid explained to the New York Times that Boyer changed his and Kaepernick's mind about the specific pose used in their protest. "We chose to kneel because it is a respectful gesture." Reid wrote in an open letter "I remember thinking our posture was like a flag flown half-mast to mark a tragedy." For those who label Kaepernick as a traitor (who hates the military), on September 1, 2016 the San Diego Chargers played a tribute to the military on the stadium video-board and Kaepernick applauded, so their words and actions dispel the lies and innuendos.

Symbolism:

Dropping to one knee is seen as a respectful gesture in war, religion, and most cultures around the world. People kneel during a loss or prayer; it's widely considered a symbol of reverence in almost any setting except in this instance (during the national anthem.) Those who deem players who take a knee as disrespectful to our troops and our country are speaking out against a gesture that a former member of our military helped popularize. Now we must ask ourselves, would a former member of our military intentionally advise players to disrespect the same flag he fought to defend? I know it to be the exact opposite, whether he agrees with the protest or not, he knows he fought for the rights of every American citizen and he advised of the most respectful way to do so.

People have tried to discredit Kaepernick for taking a knee, sporting his "pig socks," and his outward support of Castro's implementation of education within Cuba. All images have meaning. Kaepernick wore a t-shirt with Fidel's picture on it, and specifically said that he supports Castro's investment in education. When he wore the socks depicting pigs in police hats, you must understand the pigs represent "rogue cops." Pigs are considered undomesticated and often destructive or ferocious through lack of restraints or human control. Pigs are considered savages (a highly popularized term to describe cops in the 60's.) You may find fault in the depiction but the definition seems to fit.

Since Kaepernick took a knee, 1,500 plus people were killed by American Police. The problem which led to his protest continues to get worst, year after year. To discredit Kaepernick's, protest is to justify the killing of unarmed black and brown people at the hands of our police, who are here to "protect and serve," not shoot and kill. The NFL cannot claim to care about these issues if they are willing to take money that was previously allocated for other social issues in an attempt to silence and appease the players.

It would be interesting to see if the players ever exert their real power in unifying and making demands not only for 's return, but for diversity as well. Currently, there are no people of color amongst the NFL owners. For Kaepernick to not have a job is absurd; there have been players signed by teams despite the team's knowledge of the players' sketchy backgrounds or questionable actions. It boils down to the "bottom line," and most NFL owners felt like Kaepernick would affect their bottom line (as there has been a dip in television ratings.) In October of 2017, Kaepernick's lawyer filed a collusion grievance against the NFL, arguing in essence that he was "black-balled" by the owners. Colin is set to become the first star since the Vietnam era to (possibly) lose his career because of his beliefs.

Colin's Attorney, Mark Greggos, made this statement:

"If the NFL (as well as all professional sports teams) is to remain a meritocracy, then principled and peaceful protest which the owners themselves made greater theater imitating weeks ago should not be punished and athletes should not be denied employment based on partisan political provocation by the Executive Branch of our Government."

An employer cannot force their employee to parrot their political, religious, and personal views. If standing for the anthem is a form of freedom of expression, then standing or kneeling is the same one is parroting the employer's views (pro-national anthem), and the other opposes their employer's views (national anthem protest.) We must not allow these practices to exist in the public or private sector. It's the same thing as being fired or hired for vocalizing you're a republican or democrat. Imagine being discriminated against solely on the basis of your religion. You shouldn't have to mimic your employer's views; that's why we have freedom of speech in America.

NFL owners can't use profitability as their defense, as there are rules and laws put in place to prohibit such practices. The misconception being thrown out there is that this protest is hurting the NFL's bottom line, but there are active players who continue to protest, and there is no evidence linking them to loss of profits. The NFL continues to come to the aid of its players: "Our union is aware that Eric Reid and his legal representatives filed a collusion claim, which will be heard through the arbitration process, as spelled out in our collective bargain agreement." What I encourage is that the Player Union and its players start an NFL lockout, as the power is in the hands of the players, not the owners.

Amendment 1

Religious and Political Freedom

Congress shall make no law respecting and establishing or abridging the freedom of the people peaceably to assemble and to petition the government for a redress of grievances.

Kaepernick is the fruit that was born from the seed Ali planted years ago. Now a whole new generation is inspired and Kaepernick's support stockpiled:

"It baffles me that our protest is still being misconstrued as disrespect to the country, flag, and military personnel. We chose it because it's exactly the opposite. It has always been my understanding that the brave men and women who fought and died for our country did so to ensure that we could live in a fair and free society, which includes the right to speak out in protest."

-Eric Reid

"He is exercising his constitutional right and I'm glad he's doing it," Benjamin Stark, a veteran of both the U.S. Navy and U.S. Army Reserve, told Business Insider

@brennamgilmore

"My grandpa is a 97 year-old WWII Vet & Missouri farmer who wanted to join w/those who #takeaknee those kids have every right to protest."

"Colin sat down and exercised his right to protest, which is something that I feel like we all swore an oath to defend." - Tom Baker, a Navy Veteran who served in the Iraq War. "I also agree with those statements he made. We don't respect the rights of black and brown people. The whole narrative of your disrespecting Veterans and those who sacrificed is all bull."

"I am mostly just tired of pundits and nonveterans they're using us as a way to throw shade on someone for their actions." – Tom Baker

"If these people truly gave a sh-- about us veterans they would've kicked down the doors on the capital and demanded a real inquiry into the deaths at the (Department of Veterans Affairs) and the insane numbers of veterans committing suicide." – Tom Baker

Golden State Warriors Head Coach Steve Kerr:
"Kaepernick and his fellow athletes should be considered patriots. Their goal after all is to build a better, more equitable nation. Where's your heart? Where's your compassion?" Kerr added, "Whatever side of the Kaepernick issue you're on if you're helping your fellow man, that's the most important thing."
@Shawn King

"Breaking: Several Star @NFL players have told me they are considering sitting out this season until the defacto ban of Eric Reid and Colin Kaepernick is removed and both men are given spots back on rosters."

Michael Eric Dyson made a profound statement on CNN 'NEW DAY': "Even beyond Colin Kaepernick, it's bigger than him." Dyson said, "Whether or not he has flaws or virtues is the central point he's making. Many of the leaders who led us, Thomas Jefferson owned slaves; yet wrote the beautiful Declaration of Independence. We can't ask people to make perfect arguments. What we can do is ask them to be held accountable for rights we have." Dyson continued in making his point, "People once disagreed with Dr. Martin Luther King, Jr. but now celebrate his birthday every year. Times change people and people change with it."

David McGraw, owner of a Palmetto Restaurant and Ale house in Greenville, SC, stopped showing NFL games in September in his own protest. McGraw says he saw business rise 20%. Gyree Durante, a quarterback of Albright College in Reading, PA, defied the team's decision to stand and was booed for kneeling during the anthem. He says he has no regrets. "Kaepernick showed me and others around the country to fight for what you believe in." Durante says, "Don't back down." Colin Kaepernick's message, through his silent protest, has empowered others to take similar stances and not fear the consequences but to embrace the unknown and think about those who benefit from your protest while not worrying about individual consequences.

In Colin's attempt to reach a global audience, John Carlos, former track and field star who famously popularized the "Black Power Salute" at the 1968 Olympics (which prompted similar backlash) said: "I could've gone to Central Park and did it, but it never would have received the acknowledgement and created the conversations." University California Berkley Sociologist Harry Edwards who organized the 1968 Olympic protest and has advised Kaepernick, called Colin "The Muhammad Ali of his generation" and also expressed that "I'm not worried about Colin. I'm more worried about the rest of us."

The Legacy:

"If you go through life and haven't helped anybody, you haven't had much of a life." -unknown

Colin quietly donated 1 million to various charities and organizations, such as Black Lives Matter. Muhib Dyer, co-founder of the "I will not Die Young" Campaign in Milwaukee, used part of Kaepernick's $25,000 donation to buy a casket to use as a prop while addressing high schools. Colin also donated suits to "100 suits for 100 Men," a program created by Kevin Livingston that aids formerly incarcerated individuals, at-risk youth and those in need) by teaching them professionalism and the importance of being presentable for interviews by dressing formally (suit and tie.) Colin is also lending his time, attending a visit to Rikers Island with Kevin Livingston. With the considerable amount of things he is involved in, he seems like a man on a mission.

As time progressed, Kaepernick began to be inundated with praise and received more supporters. San Francisco 49ers gave Colin its most prestigious award for his contributions on and off the field, "Amnesty International Award." GQ named him their "Citizen of the Year." Time Magazine named him one of the "100 Most Influential People" in the world. The most revered award came when Sports Illustrated awarded Colin with the "Muhammad Ali Legacy" award. Colin's quest began to be a repeat of Muhammad Ali's journey but in the 21st century.

Each year Sports Illustrated and the Ali Family honors a figure who embodies the ideals of sportsmanship, leadership and philanthropy and uses his platform for changing the world. Lonnie Ali (widow of Muhammad Ali) said "I am proud to be able to present this to Colin for his passionate defense of social justice and civil rights for all people. Like Muhammad, Colin is a man who stands on his convictions with confidence and courage, undaunted by the personal sacrifices he has had to make to have his message heard. And he has used his celebrity and philanthropy to benefit our most vulnerable community members."

His legacy is yet to be fulfilled but he continues to write his own story and not allow anyone else to write it for him. Mr. Buruti explained it perfectly: "Character is the mirror to your soul. It tells what kind of person you truly are... and it's best revealed in times of difficulty and crisis because it is then that all convenience and privileges are removed." When the dust has settled, the NFL and those in opposition to Colin and the protest will be on the wrong side of history. We thank brother Kaepernick for his heroic stance - for the suffering, the pain, the love, the heartache, the willingness, and the courage. Thank You, Colin Kaepernick, for what you're doing, what you have done and what you will mean to this generation and generations that have yet to come.

"I say this as a person who receives credit for using my platform to protest systemic oppression, radicalized injustice and the dire consequences of anti-blackness of America. I accept this Award not for myself, but on behalf of the people. Because if it were not for my people, I would not be on the stage today. With or without the NFL platform, I will continue to work for the people because my platform is the people."

-Colin Kaepernick

CHAPTER 18

Open Letter

Dear Brothers and Sisters:

I pray that by the time you receive this letter, you and the relatives are well in body, mind and spirit. Tell them I send my love!

Lately I've been thinking of us as a family. I remember how close we were when we were innocent children under one roof; surviving and having fun with the little mom and pops had to offer while raising us under harsh circumstances. Although we didn't have much, we made do, and our love for each other was so very pure. I think it was pure because we didn't love each other based upon what we wanted from each other... shoot, we didn't have nothing! (you know what I mean, material things) we were broke! But we had love! We always wanted each other to at least taste a piece of the pie (and moms made some good pie didn't she?) I miss that spirit mom and pops instilled in us. We owe them more out of our lives.

What I mean is that it seems as though we got caught up in our own individual lives as we got older. I know we still love each other and we got our own families and responsibilities and all that good stuff, but man it seems as though we can do more. We have to do more.

I remember when one of us had a problem or someone picked on one of our sisters or brothers, we were ALL there! Not just a couple of us but ALL OF US showed up to the fight! Man, it used to be like "What y'all want!? A Battle Royale out here! (ha, ha)... We was that tight and connected. We couldn't be touched when we rolled like that... connected!

Nowadays some of us have too much pride and ego to call on each other when times get hard. Everybody has their own agenda, and that's cool, but when one part of the body is infected or incapacitated the rest of the body becomes deficient in some form or fashion. Remember VOLTRON? We use to watch it all the time. Back then I was caught up into the action hero stuff, the kid side of cartoons. When I became a man, I realized the true concept behind the cartoon. The protection and maintenance of the whole is essential in overcoming obstacles. So, if any of you are up against a difficulty think about how VOLTRON use to unite when a task was at hand.

I know individually we all are doing well financially and some of us are even global icons, can you believe that? But do y'all remember that last talk grandma and granddad had with us before they passed? "Don't you ever rate yourself based on material or financial gains in life. It's an illusion. Rate yourselves on how you fight and stand to ensure your brothers and sisters never have to suffer what our ancestors suffered through. You children will one day come to understand more when you get older, and when you come to understand and live by what we're saying to you, you will all be rich in ways you cannot perceive right now..." I think about that seed of wisdom they dropped on our little fertile brains back then and have come to realize this: They were passing down something deeply ingrained in our family and in our people throughout our history and passed down amongst a long line of generations that says we should never forget where we came from or think we "made it" when the rest of our family or people may be suffering.

When I think about their words my heart pains me. I guess they forecast the changing of the times and illusions that society would place in front of us to cause us to FORGET the reality that our ancestors faced for centuries.

I aint trying to get all "deep" and all that either (ha, ha), but y'all know me, I've always been prone to look deep into things. I guess that's why y'all always call me when you need to figure something out! (Ha, ha). Seriously though, I love y'all and I'm ready to live like we did back under the same roof again. Loving, struggling, protecting, fighting and doing whatever it takes for ALL OF US to have a bite at that pie! Living by the principles mom, pops, grandma, grandad and our ancestors passed on many years ago for us to live by...

Love Always,
Your fam!
P.S.

Just to remind you all that we have a family reunion coming around. We all need to show up. There are many issues affecting our family that need to be discussed and action taken to repair. All of us have to pitch in somehow. The survival and legacy of our family is vital. All personal agendas should be sidelined (for the moment) as the unity and upliftment of the whole is reestablished and secured.

Again,

Love, Your Fam...

Note: The authors of this book used a wide variety of publications to assist them in the formulation of their ideas. Listed here are the sources that were specific (general, historical, and factual) to passages in the book.

Cleaver, Eldridge, *Soul on Ice,* New York, Random House, 1968, page 52

D, Chuck, *Fight the Power (Rap, Race and Reality),* United Kingdom, Payback Press, 1997

Fanon, Frantz, *The Wretched of the Earth,* New York, Grove Press, Inc., 1965, pages 81 & 82

Harris, Brookshire, *Billionaire Branding,* Brookshire Book Group, 2016, page 82

Jackson, George, *Soledad brothers,* Chicago, Lawrence Hill Books (Chicago Review Press), 1994, *pages* 108 & 179

Kilgore, James, Understanding *Mass Incarceration,* New York, The New Press, 2015, page 59

Lynch, Willie, *Willie Lynch letter: The Making of a Slave,* (Original publication date 1712), Final Call, 2009, http://www.finalcall.com/artman/publish/Perspectives_1/ Willie_Lynch_letter_The_Making_of_a_Slave.shtml

Rose, Jenn *How much money do private prisons make,* Romper, 2016, https://www.romper.com/p/how-much-money-do-private-prisons-make-theyre-earning-thousands-per-inmate-16680

Seale, Bobby, *Seize the Time,* Baltimore, Black Classic Press, 1991, page 108

Toland, John, *Adolph Hitler,* New York, Knopf Doubleday Publishing Group (Anchor), 1991, page 19

Welsing, Dr. Francis Cress, *The Isis Papers: The Keys to the Colors,* Chicago, Third World Press, 1991, pages 45 & 81

Wilson, Amos, *Blueprint for Black Power: A Moral, Political and Economic Imperative for the Twenty-First Century,* New York, Afrikan World InfoSystems, 2005, page 108

Windsor, Rudolph. R *The Valley of Dry Bones: The Conditions that Black People face in America Today,* Atlanta, Windsor's Golden Series, 1988, page 117

Woodson, Carter. G, *The Mis-Education of the Negro,* (Place of publication not identified), Start Publishing LLC, 2013, page 117

ABOUT THE AUTHORS

LORENZO "S.DOT" STEPHENS IS AN
AFRICAN-AMERICAN MALE FROM
RICHMOND, VIRGINIA.

ALFRED "SAEED" RIVERA
IS A PUERTORICAN-AMERICAN MALE
FROM BROOKLYN, NEW YORK.

MIKEY "MAGNETIC" MOMBRANCHE
IS A HAITIAN-AMERICAN MALE FROM
POMPANO BEACH, FLORIDA

BEVERLEY SMITH IS A BIRACIAL
FEMALE FROM THE UK, WHO
CURRENTLY RESIDESIN GERMANY.

Order Form

MAKE CHECKS AND MONEY ORDERS PAYABLE TO:

QUESTIONS OR COMMENTS CONTACT US AT:
EMAIL: THEMOVEMENTINC4@GMAIL.COM
FACEBOOK: THEMOVEMENTINC4
TWITTER: @INC4THE

Name:_____
Address:_____
City:_____ State:_____
Zip:_____

Amount		Book Title or Pen Pal Number	Price
		Included for shipping for 1 book	**$4 U.S. / $9 Inter**

This book can also be purchased on:
AMAZON.COM/
BARNES&NOBLE.COM/CREATESPACE.COM